ADVANCE PRAISE
FOR OPPORTUNITY AT RISK

"This book provides a vital framework for leaders committed to long-term value creation in both private businesses and institutional portfolios. At Sovereign's Capital, we partner with faith-driven management teams to steward resources responsibly and to pursue enduring operational and financial excellence, not short-term gains; the insights in this book reinforce the discipline required to identify and mitigate risks that can erode that pursuit over time. For our portfolio company leaders, applying these principles will strengthen strategic execution and resilience in the face of uncertainty. For fund managers and investors, the book underscores the importance of holistic risk awareness in capital allocation decisions, aligning investment theses with sustainable competitive advantages and disciplined stewardship. This is essential reading for anyone focused on building durable enterprises and investment outcomes that serve both performance and purpose."

Michael Tremain
Managing Partner, Private Equity, Sovereign's Capital

"Long-term success in wealth management is less about forecasting returns and more about understanding how decisions compound under stress. *Opportunity at Risk* reframes risk as a strategic discipline, one that must be evaluated across capital, behavior, governance, and time. This book offers families and advisors a practical way to pressure-test their strategies before markets, lawsuits, or life events do it for them. It's a thoughtful and necessary contribution to how enduring wealth is actually managed."

John Chatmas
Chief Executive Officer, Waterloo Capital

"Over the past decade, I have worked directly with Warren as he implemented the Total Family Balance Sheet framework to manage risk across my family office, business, and personal life. What makes this model so powerful is not its theory, but its execution, it forces you to identify risks that typically remain hidden, understand how they cascade across personal and business domains, and make deliberate decisions about what to avoid, mitigate, transfer, or assume. I have seen firsthand how this approach materially reduces blind spots, strengthens decision-making, and prevents single events from becoming catastrophic outcomes. This book accurately reflects the discipline Warren has applied for years, and it should be required reading for successful families, business owners and leaders who want a proactive integrated risk management framework, not an after-the-fact solutions when something goes wrong."

Jeff Metzler
Chief Executive Officer, Lone Star Electric Supply

"This book brings clarity to an often-overlooked reality: enduring family continuity and leadership effectiveness are driven by disciplined, holistic risk management across every dimension of a family's holdings, which extends much further than just the operating business(es). For more than fifteen years, I have leveraged Warren's advice as he served as a mentor and active risk manager to my family and I, helping surface interconnected risks spanning businesses, personal assets, investments, and human capital. His approach consistently challenged fragmented thinking and replaced it with coordinated, intentional decision-making, oftentimes missed by even the most seasoned professional. That same framework is clearly articulated in this book. At Clear Companies, we emphasize culture, purpose, human flourishment, alignment, accountability, and long-term stewardship; this model extends those principles beyond the organization and into the broader family office ecosystem. This is essential reading for families and leaders who want to protect what they have built and what they have been blessed with, anticipate risk before it becomes loss, and create resilience that endures across generations."

Cale Kobza
Chief Executive Officer, Clear Companies

OPPORTUNITY at RISK

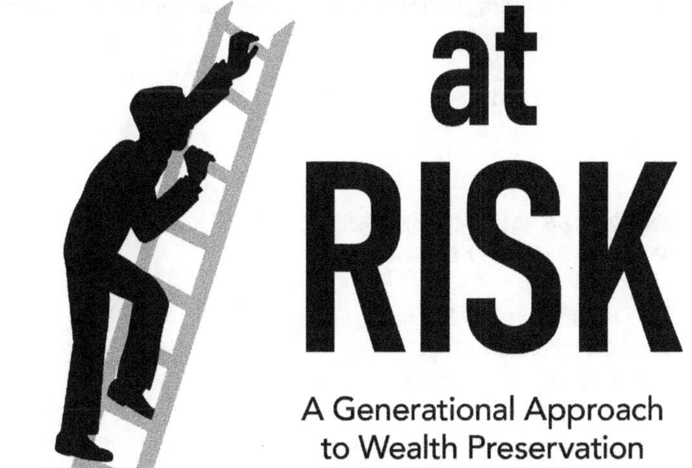

A Generational Approach
to Wealth Preservation
Through Comprehensive
Risk Management

WARREN E. BARHORST

with **DAVID A. GOLDBERG** and
DAVID K. HOLLINGSWORTH

Published by Performance Publishing, Charleston, South Carolina.
An imprint of Advantage Media.

Performance Publishing is a registered trademark, and the Performance Publishing colophon is a trademark of Advantage Media.

Printed in the United States of America.

10 9 8 7 6 5 4 3 2 1

ISBN: 978-1-967451-48-7 (Paperback)
ISBN: 978-1-967451-09-8 (Hardcover)

Cover Design by Brenda Melgar.
Interior Art by Brenda Melgar.
Layout design by Ronald Pono.

Performance Publishing is an imprint of Advantage Media Group. Advantage Media helps busy entrepreneurs, CEOs, and leaders write and publish a book to grow their business and become the authority in their field. Performance Publishing authors comprise a community of industry professionals, idea-makers, and thought leaders. For more information, go to performancepublishinggroup.com.

WHAT YOU DON'T SEE CAN COST YOU EVERYTHING

OPPORTUNITY at RISK

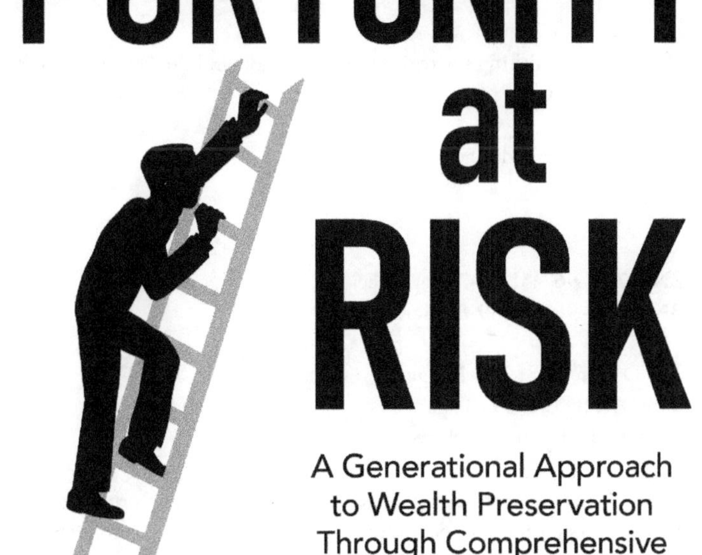

A Generational Approach
to Wealth Preservation
Through Comprehensive
Risk Management

WARREN E. BARHORST

WITH **DAVID A. GOLDBERG** AND
DAVID K. HOLLINGSWORTH

Published by Performance Publishing, Charleston, South Carolina.
An imprint of Advantage Media.

Performance Publishing is a registered trademark, and the Performance Publishing colophon is a trademark of Advantage Media.

Printed in the United States of America.

10 9 8 7 6 5 4 3 2 1

ISBN: 978-1-967451-48-7 (Paperback)
ISBN: 978-1-967451-09-8 (Hardcover)

Cover Design by Brenda Melgar.
Interior Art by Brenda Melgar.
Layout design by Ronald Pono.

Performance Publishing is an imprint of Advantage Media Group. Advantage Media helps busy entrepreneurs, CEOs, and leaders write and publish a book to grow their business and become the authority in their field. Performance Publishing authors comprise a community of industry professionals, idea-makers, and thought leaders. For more information, go to performancepublishinggroup.com.

ABOUT THE AUTHORS

Warren E. Barhorst, CPRIA®, ACPRIA®, CAPI®, LUTCF®, FSCP®

Warren E. Barhorst is an entrepreneur, author, investor, and nationally recognized leader in risk management, insurance, and financial services, with more than three decades of experience building, scaling, and advising successful enterprises. Over the course of his career, Warren has been involved as a founder, investor, or strategic partner in more than 20 entrepreneurial companies, spanning insurance, financial services, real estate, consulting, and emerging ventures.

He is the founder of Iscential, a private risk management and financial services firm he launched in 1993 and grew into a multi-state organization serving high-net-worth individuals and complex businesses. In 2023, Iscential became a partner firm of Higginbotham, where Warren continues as a Managing Partner.

Throughout his career, Warren has been known for setting clear vision, designing scalable distribution strategies, and developing high-performance leadership cultures. He has led organizations from startup to national prominence, managed large-scale P&L and balance sheets, and advised companies ranging from early-stage ventures to Fortune 100 firms. His expertise spans enterprise risk management, captive insurance, financial strategy, taxation efficiency, mergers and acquisitions, and organizational growth.

Warren is the author of two business books in the *Game Plan* series. His first, ***Game Plan...The Definitive Playbook for Starting and***

Growing Your Business, provides a practical framework for entrepreneurs building sustainable companies from the ground up. His second book, ***Game Plan...The Definitive Playbook for Selling in the Connection Culture***, explores modern sales leadership, trust-based relationships, and how authentic connection drives long-term growth in today's marketplace. Together, these works reflect Warren's belief that strong strategy, disciplined execution, and people-centered leadership are inseparable.

A graduate of Texas A&M University, where he earned a Bachelor of Science in Industrial Distribution and lettered in football, Warren remains deeply committed to education and mentorship. He has served on numerous corporate, nonprofit, and university boards, including the Texas A&M Mays Business School Advisory Board and the University of Houston Wolff Center for Entrepreneurship.

His leadership and companies have earned widespread recognition, including induction into the Nationwide Insurance Agent Hall of Fame, Ernst & Young Entrepreneur of the Year honors, multiple "Best Places to Work" awards, and repeated inclusion on the Inc. 5000 and Aggie 100 lists.

Today, Warren continues to invest, consult, write, and speak on risk management, entrepreneurship, leadership, and sustainable business growth, bringing a practitioner's perspective shaped by decades of building companies, managing risk, developing people, and executing strategy at the highest levels.

David A. Goldberg

David A. Goldberg is a Managing Director at Higginbotham and a trusted advisor to entrepreneurs, executives, and families navigating complex wealth, risk, estate, and business planning decisions. His perspective is shaped by an uncommon combination of operating experience, capital markets exposure, and deep risk management insight. Rather than viewing wealth as a collection of isolated assets, David approaches it as an interconnected system, one that must be intentionally structured, actively protected, and continuously adapted as it grows.

Before entering financial services, David spent years as an entrepreneur and operator, building, scaling, and investing in businesses across multiple industries. As a venture-backed founder, he led and participated in teams that raised eight figures of institutional capital and achieved successful exits, including transactions involving companies such as Penske Media and AOL. These experiences gave him firsthand exposure to liquidity events, concentrated equity risk, governance challenges, reputational exposure, and the cascading consequences that arise when growth outpaces risk planning. He has lived the reality that wealth creation often introduces new vulnerabilities long before families recognize they exist.

Following the successful exit of his most recent venture, an AI-powered telehealth platform in the integrative medicine space, David made a deliberate transition into financial services. He was drawn to work that required integrating investments, insurance, legal structures, and family governance into a coordinated strategy. His background as an operator allows him to engage clients not only as an advisor, but as someone who understands the emotional complexity and real-world tradeoffs inherent when personal wealth, family legacy, and business risk intersect.

David's advisory philosophy reflects the core principles of the Total Family Balance Sheet framework. He emphasizes disciplined risk evaluation, coordinated professional collaboration, and thoughtful execution over reactive planning. He frequently works alongside attorneys, CPAs, investment advisors, and family office professionals to ensure strategies are integrated, durable, and adaptable as circumstances evolve.

Today, David's practice centers on holistic planning and advanced risk management, with particular emphasis on identifying off-balance-sheet liabilities, aligning risk strategies across asset silos, and helping families balance growth with protection. His work spans estate and gift planning, insurance design, asset protection, business succession, and family governance, always viewed through the lens of how a single unmanaged risk can ripple across the entire family balance sheet.

David K. Hollingsworth, CPCU®, CLU®, FMLI®

David K. Hollingsworth is a seasoned insurance executive, board leader, and business coach with more than four decades of experience in the insurance and financial services industry. He is a retired Senior Vice President of Nationwide Insurance, where he held a variety of leadership roles and developed a reputation for strategic thinking, operational discipline, and principled leadership.

In addition to his corporate leadership career, David has served as Chairman of the Board of Directors for Iscential Insurance, providing governance and strategic oversight in a rapidly evolving distribution environment. For more than 20 years, he has coached insurance agencies, financial advisory firms, and related businesses, helping leaders navigate growth, succession, risk management, and organizational change.

He is currently an active board member/chairman of several businesses where he provides ongoing management support. David also has a consulting firm designed to help business leaders make their dreams a reality. He is a shareholder of Higginbotham and provides advisory services as needed.

David holds an MBA from Drake University and is a graduate of the University of Iowa. He has earned several of the industry's most respected professional designations, including CPCU (Chartered Property Casualty Underwriter), CLU (Chartered Life Underwriter), and FMLI (Fellow, Life Management Institute), reflecting both technical expertise and a deep commitment to professional excellence.

David's writing draws on real-world experience rather than theory alone. He focuses on practical insights, sound decision-making, and long-term value creation, particularly at the intersection of leadership, strategy, and risk. His approach is thoughtful, direct, and grounded in the belief that sustainable success comes from clarity, discipline, and integrity.

The Role of Artificial Intelligence in Developing This Book

Artificial intelligence played a meaningful supporting role in the creation of this book, serving as a powerful tool for brainstorming, refining discussion points, fact-checking concepts, and exploring complex ideas from multiple angles. While every insight and conclusion reflects the authors independent judgment and professional experience, AI provided an efficient way to pressure-test assumptions, expand perspectives, and enhance clarity throughout the writing process. Used responsibly and thoughtfully, AI acted not as a substitute for expertise but as a collaborative accelerant, helping transform raw concepts into a more comprehensive and accessible resource for families, advisors, and practitioners.

A Note to the Reader

This book and its contents do not constitute investment, legal, or tax advice of any kind nor should they operate as a substitute for the services of any investment, legal or tax professional.

The Role of Artificial Intelligence in Developing This Book

Artificial intelligence played a meaningful supporting role in the creation of this book, serving as a powerful tool for brainstorming, refining discussion points, fact-checking concepts, and exploring complex ideas from multiple angles. While every insight and conclusion reflects the authors independent judgment and professional experience, AI provided an efficient way to pressure-test assumptions, expand perspectives, and enhance clarity throughout the writing process. Used responsibly and thoughtfully, AI acted not as a substitute for expertise but as a collaborative accelerant, helping transform raw concepts into a more comprehensive and accessible resource for families, advisors, and practitioners.

A Note to the Reader

This book and its contents do not constitute investment, legal, or tax advice of any kind nor should they operate as a substitute for the services of any investment, legal or tax professional.

CONTENTS

My Journey to the Total Family Balance Sheet

This preface details the author's journey in developing the **Off-balance-sheet-liabilities** of the Total Family Balance Sheet, highlighting the limitations of traditional wealth and risk management approaches and the need for a holistic, integrated framework.

PART I

The Framework – Understanding and Anticipating the Risks Associated with Wealth Accumulation and Preservation

Chapter 1

An Introduction to Holistic Wealth and Risk Management

This chapter introduces holistic wealth and risk management, emphasizing the necessity of coordinated efforts across Asset Silos to effectively safeguard families against potential catastrophic financial losses and preserve wealth.

Chapter 2

Introducing the Total Family Balance Sheet Framework

This chapter presents the Total Family Balance Sheet framework, which evaluates both assets and unaccounted liabilities across six key silos, enabling families to comprehensively assess their overall financial well-being and more effectively plan for future generations.

Chapter 3

Why Managing Risk Matters Now More Than Ever

This chapter highlights the pressing need for comprehensive risk management in today's volatile economic environment, characterized by macroeconomic instability, natural disasters, and social inflation, and urges families to adopt a proactive and holistic approach to long-term financial management.

PART II

Exposures of The Six Asset Silos of the Total Family Balance Sheet Framework

This chapter examines the challenges and risks faced by family-owned businesses, highlighting the importance of succession planning and proactive risk assessments in achieving long-term success and stability.

This chapter explores the complexities and risks associated with private equity investments, highlighting the importance of Informed decision-making and robust risk management strategies specific to private equity (PE) and venture capital (VC) investments, to better align with family objectives.

This chapter addresses the unique risks associated with personal assets and emphasizes the necessity of tailored risk management strategies to safeguard this often-overlooked financially material and emotional asset class.

This chapter highlights the critical value of family human capital, examining how skills, relationships, and governance influence a family's financial well-being and long-term legacy.

PART III

Implementing the Total Family Balance Sheet

This concluding chapter highlights the significance of the Total Family Balance Sheet framework in achieving comprehensive preservation and the perpetuation of family wealth ultimately helping to safeguard families against the gravitational forces that threaten their financial legacy.

A LETTER FROM THE AUTHOR

My Journey to the Total Family Balance Sheet

This book recounts my journey toward innovating a revolutionary concept: **Managing the Risk of the Total Family Balance Sheet.**

For decades, as a licensed **Risk Manager**, I witnessed the limitations of a traditional approach to wealth and risk management. Asset growth and risk management were often treated as separate or even competing goals. The result was lopsided strategies, either chasing aggressive returns while neglecting safeguards or overcorrecting with excessive risk aversion. This fragmented approach, I realized, was inadequate for the complex realities facing successful families, whether their net worth is $1 million or $1 billion.

My "aha!" moment came from observing this dichotomy in practice and seeking a better way forward for my clients.

In 2019, after 25 years of working with clients, this challenge remained the most persistent thorn in my side. Seeking answers, I turned to the Continuing Education Department at the Wharton School of Business at the University of Pennsylvania. Since 1955, Wharton's Wealth Management Initiative has been the United States longest continual study of family wealth and perpetuation designed to educate and better equip advisors, investors, fiduciaries, families, and policymakers. Fortunately, CHUBB

Insurance nominated and sponsored me to attend this program under their Certified Advisor of Private Insurance (CAPI) designation.

The one-year program was led by Dr. Christopher Geczy. Dr. Geczy, a long-time faculty member at Wharton (since 1997), holds a B.A. in Economics from the University of Pennsylvania and a PhD in Econometrics from the Graduate School of Business at the University of Chicago. During my time in the program, he served as Academic Director of the Wealth Management Institute at Wharton.

Figure 0.1 Geczy "aha" Moment: Dr. Christopher Geczy's six-asset-class model at Wharton sparks the realization that unaccounted for liabilities must be given equal weight with assets on the Total Family Balance Sheet.

It was in this course that I encountered his life's work in developing the Total Family Balance Sheet. I began pairing this with my own experience in managing risk, especially Off-balance-sheet-liabilities that often go unaccounted for and can significantly damage a family's asset base. These liabilities, although not typically reflected on a traditional balance sheet, must be recognized and planned for. Together, these liabilities equate to a family's total liabilities.

Dr. Geczy's focus had primarily been on "chasing alpha" or beating the market benchmarks while managing economic and other financial-related exposures. He created a model outlining the six asset classes most successful high net worth families hold. When I saw this, I wrote on my notes: *"Need a way to illustrate the Off-balance-sheet-liabilities on the Total Family Balance Sheet."* This became my mission and ultimately the foundation of my capstone presentation at Wharton in December of 2019.

This framework is the same structure that should be used for risk management. Still, it also requires an added layer of coordination among professionals to provide optimal protection for family assets, wealth accumulation, and generational wealth transfer.

Dr. Geczy often referred to applying the "Laws of Physics" to wealth accumulation and preservation: namely, the principle of **Financial Gravity.** In his model, Financial Gravity represents the ongoing drag on net worth, encompassing sources such as spending, inflation, taxation, and losses, all forces that can naturally reduce an asset base over time. The reality is, without proactive comprehensive growth and risk management, wealth tends to dissipate over time.

Figure 0.2 Financial Gravity: Newton's apple becomes a metaphor for the constant downward force of spending, inflation, taxation, losses, etc, all which can dissipate family wealth if left unmanaged.

While I found the model compelling, I felt it was missing a key component. I have witnessed firsthand how one major event, or a series of small ones, can be catastrophic to the net worth of families that has been built over years. The issue has historically been, that there is an immense, coordinated focus on asset growth with limited or no attention paid to risk management of the assets, much less coordination across the management of the six **Asset Silos.**

At one point, Dr. Geczy posed a question: 'How many of the original Forbes 400 list from 1982 are still on the list today? 300? 100?'

The answer, according to a 2022 Forbes article by Sarah Thomas Oxtoby, was just 17. That's right, only 17 families remain from the original list, underscoring how difficult it is to sustain wealth across generations.

He also shared a quote from Andrew Carnegie that stuck with me:

"Three generations from shirtsleeves to shirtsleeves."

I wondered if this was a uniquely American phenomenon?

A quick Google search revealed otherwise:

- *"Rice paddy to rice paddy."* (Japan)
- *"Clog to clog."* (The Netherlands)
- *"Stables to stars back to stables."* (England)
- *"He who doesn't have it, does it, and he who has it, misuses it"* (Spain)

Across cultures, the message is clear: wealth, if not nurtured across generations, often dissipates.

These proverbs emphasize the importance of families staying connected, not just financially, but also in terms of values and purpose. Managing the Total Family Balance Sheet isn't just about wealth accumulation and perpetuation; it's about the strength and stability of the family over generations.

Families with less wealth are only afforded a few mistakes. Families with more net worth may be able to absorb more hits, but those hits can be exponentially more damaging. As the Forbes list shows, no one is immune to the reality of Financial Gravity. The Forbes 400 list shows us only 5% of America's wealthiest families since 1982 have been able to defy Financial Gravity, truly propelling wealth through generations.

That was when it became clear that an asset growth strategy alone wasn't enough. For a truly effective strategy, an asset growth and risk management framework must be insightful comprehensive, and complementary in nature. This book shares how we built and execute on that framework one capable of integrating every element of a family's financial life: investments, real estate, family businesses, private equity investments, personal assets, and critical family human capital.

With these additions, *The Total Family Balance Sheet by Higginbotham*™ was born from the real-world consequences of fragmented approaches to wealth and risk management. The application of this framework isn't just theoretical. Since 2019, we've used this off-balance-sheet liability focused framework with clients to improve their financial planning, succession strategy, and most importantly their peace of mind.

Why This Book Matters

The chapters that follow outline the Total Family Balance Sheet Framework for you and your advisors to implement in your family planning, just as we have supported countless clients in doing so. There will be a deep dive into the variables that drive the four core principles of *The Total Family Balance Sheet by Higginbotham*™: holistic view, Informed risk evaluation, intergenerational wealth transfer, and values alignment. You'll see what we've learned by watching families succeed, and fail, at maintaining wealth across generations.

Some skillfully navigated generations of wealth. Others fell victim to unforeseen circumstances or events. This framework effectively bridges the gap between proactive risk management and strategic growth, paving the way for truly holistic wealth accumulation and preservation.

Figure 0.3 Knights of the Round Table Example*: The most successful families implement a team approach to wealth accumulation and preservation leveraging their expertise and coordinating implementation across their advisory team.*

The Total Family Balance Sheet by Higginbotham™ focuses on optimizing assets and identifying risks, building a legacy of financial resilience and safeguarding the future well-being of families facing the complexities of wealth in a constantly evolving world.

The development of *The Total Family Balance Sheet by Higginbotham*™ represents a fundamental shift in overall wealth management thinking. This paradigm prioritizes both growth and protection, offering a powerful new lens for understanding, organizing, and protecting family wealth across generations.

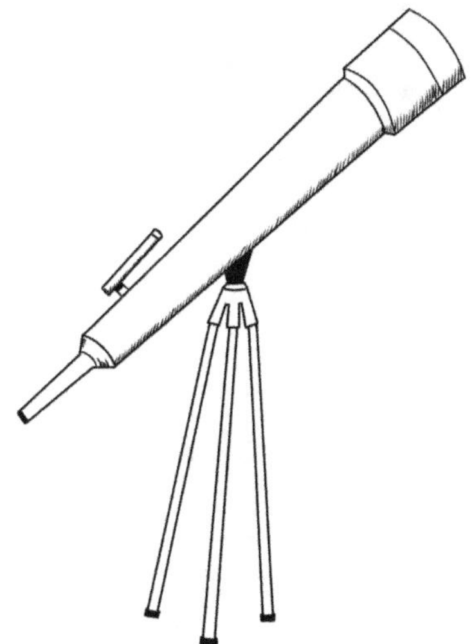

Figure 0.4 Reframing Lens: The "lens" graphic illustrates how The Total Family Balance Sheet by Higginbotham™ offers families an intensified, clear, and integrated view of every asset, liability, and risk.

May you defy gravity,

Warren E. Barhorst

PART I

THE FRAMEWORK

UNDERSTANDING AND ANTICIPATING THE RISKS ASSOCIATED WITH WEALTH ACCUMULATION AND PRESERVATION

This section defines the core problems families face today: why traditional wealth management often fails, how unmanaged risk compounds over time, and what is required to protect and preserve a lasting legacy.

It introduces *The Total Family Balance Sheet by Higginbotham*™ as a modern, coordinated approach to wealth and risk management, designed to integrate assets, exposures, and decisions across every aspect of a family's financial life.

By aligning strategy across Asset Silos and evaluating Informed versus Uninformed risks using consistent tools and terminology, this framework empowers families to proactively manage the forces of Financial Gravity that can erode wealth over generations.

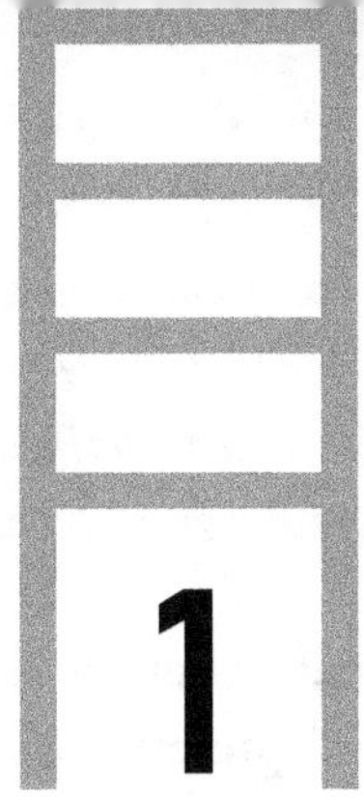

THE WHOLE PICTURE

An Introduction to Holistic Wealth and Risk Management

For generations, wealth management has often operated in silos, with risk management even more so. Financial advisors have typically focused on asset growth, while insurance professionals, attorneys, and other specialists have addressed risk management independently, often without coordination.

This fragmented approach may suffice for simpler financial situations, but it falls drastically short for successful individuals and families navigating the complexities of modern wealth management. This chapter introduces a revolutionary alternative: Holistic wealth and risk management.

Beyond Asset Growth: A Paradigm Shift

Traditional approaches to wealth management have primarily emphasized asset growth, focusing on maximizing returns on investments through diversified portfolios and strategic asset allocation. While undeniably important, this singular focus often overlooks an equally critical component: risk management.

Consider the classic scenario: a portfolio expertly crafted for maximizing returns, yet completely vulnerable to a single catastrophic event, such as a lawsuit or a major health crisis. The gains painstakingly accumulated over time can vanish overnight, rendering the growth-focused strategy futile.

Holistic wealth and risk management moves beyond this narrow view. It acknowledges that true wealth preservation requires both the accumulation and strategic protection of assets. It's a paradigm shift, moving away from a fragmented approach towards a unified, integrated strategy that places equal emphasis on both asset growth and risk management.

Direct Private Equity Investment Without Operational Risk Managemt Review

Consider a successful family that chooses to diversify by funding a modest direct private equity investment with a friend or relative. They complete due diligence on the opportunity's return potential but neglect to examine the business's Operational Risk.

By overlooking these Off-balance-sheet-liabilities, the family exposes itself to significant risk. If the company encounters an adverse event, the family could lose its invested capital, face liability exposure, and suffer reputational damage, depleting both financial and family human capital.

The Inverted Risk Focus

To begin, how most families view risk is upside down, literally. Most families tend to have an **Inverted Risk Focus**, spending an inordinate amount of time, energy, and money protecting against rare risks, while often overlooking the more likely, and sometimes inevitable, ones.

Fire Risk vs. Flooding Risk

Many families prioritize purchasing fire insurance for their homes, even though statistically they are 10 times more likely to experience a flooding event.

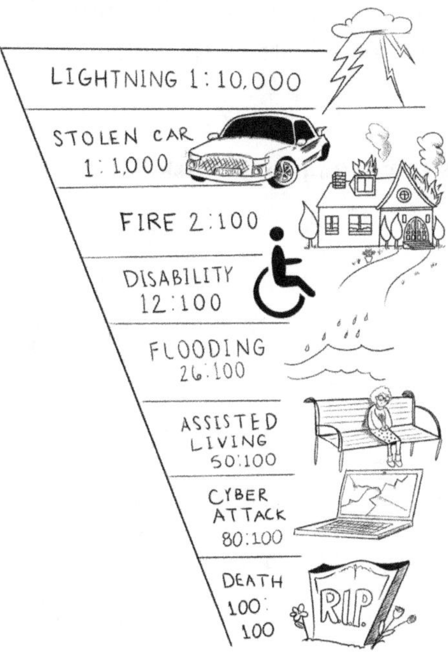

Figure 1.1 The Inverted Risk Focus: *Families over-prepare for rare risks while ignoring more likely threats.*

Lightning Strikes vs. Everyday Threats

When a storm approaches a sporting event, practice, or golf course, everything comes to a halt. Players and spectators are rushed to safety, even though the odds of being struck by lightning in an 80-year lifespan are just 1 in 10,000.[1] It is estimated that, on average, the United States has over 240 million lightning strikes with an annual average of 22 fatalities. Based on National Weather Service data, the annual odds of an individual in the United States dying from a lightning strike are approximately 1 in 16 million.

This is not to diminish the importance of lightning safety. Rather, it highlights the broader issue: families often misallocate their focus, emphasizing improbable dangers while ignoring far more likely risks.

---

[1] *Cooper, Mary Ann, and Ronald L. Holle. "Lightning Injuries." StatPearls, StatPearls Publishing, 2024, www.ncbi.nlm.nih.gov/books/NBK441920/.*

The Total Family Balance Sheet framework aims to realign this perspective, enabling families to evaluate and prioritize risks based on **Frequency** and **Severity**.

We refer to this as a "**Foundational Risk**" approach:

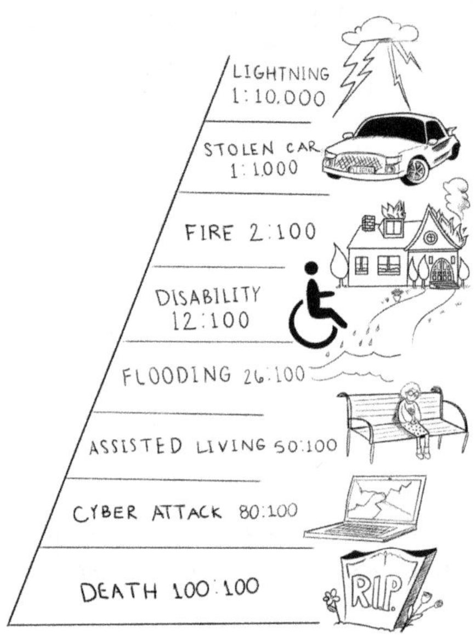

Figure 1.2 Foundational Risk Approach: Focus risk strategy on events most likely and most damaging.

While these examples are illustrative, each family must determine what is truly foundational to their specific wealth story.

To properly assess and prioritize risks, families should consider two key variables.

- **Frequency:** How likely is the event to occur? (e.g., a fender bender is common; a lightning strike is rare.)
- **Severity:** What would be the financial and emotional impact if it did occur? (Is it annoying or catastrophic?)

When paired with the family's specific **Risk Tolerance**, this lens enables a more strategic, personalized, and efficient approach to risk management.

Family & Advisor Roles

Silo Disconnect and the Missing Risk Manager

When viewed through the lens of the asset side of the balance sheet, the six silos of wealth management, investments, real estate, family operating business, private equity, personal assets, and family human capital are typically managed in isolation. Professionals responsible for these silos often operate independently, with little to no communication between themselves.

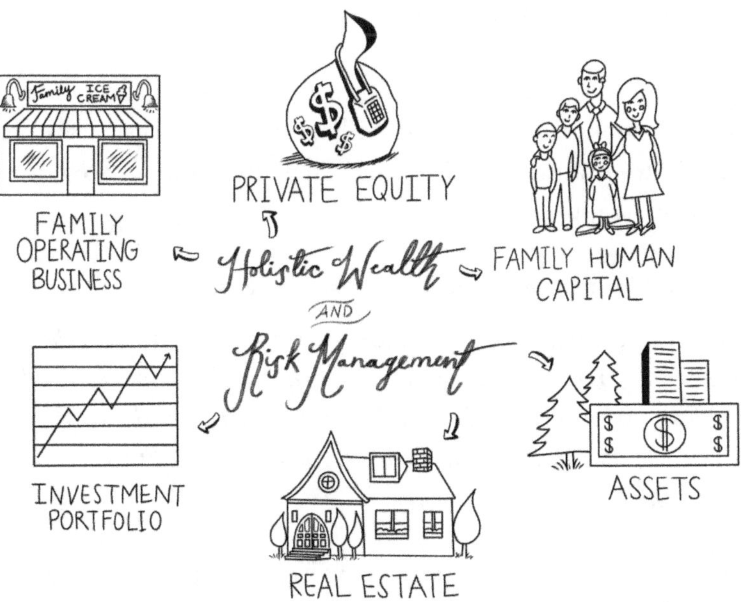

Figure 1.3 Silo Disconnect in Wealth Management: Professionals manage silos independently, leaving risk coordination gaps.

While these professionals are usually highly skilled in driving asset growth, the risks associated with their activities are often treated as background noise, handled as part of the business as usual.

What's missing?

A dedicated approach to Risk Management.

A directive to all of the families' advisors to look across the asset silos, identify interdependencies, and actively coordinate risk management strategies through a designated family office risk leader, or centralized risk management team that has the responsibility and authority to understand, monitor, and manage risk across the full balance sheet, with the expectation that someone is getting up everyday focused specifically on risk.

In today's complex financial environment, an integrated, professional approach to risk management is required. Without this, families remain vulnerable to blind spots, adverse events that result in catastrophic losses across multiple areas of their financial life.

A fragmented and uncoordinated approach to risk management especially one that overlooks Off-balance-sheet-liabilities, frequently leaves families exposed to devastating consequences. These breakdowns are not theoretical; they often appear in the news.

Ice Cream Manufacturer and the Listeria Outbreak

In 2015, a well-known ice cream manufacturer suffered a listeria outbreak. The event triggered a massive product recall, resulting in a severe financial crisis. Ultimately, the family was forced to sell the business in a fire sale to an outside investor. To make matters worse, the CEO was indicted on seven counts.

This real-world example illustrates how one family's operating business, with siloed risk management, suffered a complete collapse. The ripple effects were likely emense, with stress from the family operating business likely spilling over into other asset silos pulling them down with it. In situations like this, it is also likely that the family's human capital took a serious hit from the reputational fallout, while personal assets were also most likely strained or depleted in an effort to stabilize the damage and absorb the aftermath.

Figure 1.4 The Listeria Collapse: *A real-world example of unmanaged risk decimating a family business.*

Unfortunately, stories like this are far too common. Most families reach their "aha!" moment, recognizing the weaknesses of their risk management strategy after it's too late.

The goal of the Total Family Balance Sheet framework, and the reason this book exists, is to motivate families, individuals, and business owners to take proactive steps. By developing and maintaining a coordinated and **Integrated Risk Management** strategy, they can protect their assets, shield their reputation, and offset the long-term gravitational forces that threaten their net worth.

Governance, Communication, and The Limitations of Bifurcated Risk Management

Figure 1.5 The Cost of Fragmentation: Limitations of uncoordinated, siloed risk management.

Traditional, siloed approaches to risk management often falls short, especially for families with complex financial lives. This fragmented model leads to critical gaps for several reasons.

Lack of Coordination

Professionals such as insurance agents, wealth advisors, family office managers, business operators, lawyers, and tax specialists typically operate independently within their respective areas of expertise within their designated Asset Silo. This isolation can create dangerous overlaps, gaps, or outright blind spots in risk coverage.

Imagine a family *who improperly structured their $50M buy/sell life insurance inside of the company, which is owned in their taxable estate, not accounting for the United States vs. Connelly decision, inadvertently adding an additional $50M to the valuation of the company at the owner's untimely death, ultimately increasing the family's estate tax liability by $20M.*[2]

Had the advisors been in coordination and had transparency into the family's business succession plan and estate plan, the life insurance to fund the buy/sell agreement could have been held in a separate entity not impacting the valuation of the business, thus so, not having an impact on the family's estate tax liability.

Incomplete Risk Assessment

Taking a fragmented approach often fails to address the interconnected nature of modern risk.

For example, *a family operating company is in a lawsuit stemming from an act of negligence that led to a fatal accident. The lawsuit might bring not only financial strain, and stress, to the operating business of the family but also reputational harm to the family's human capital. The publicity of the incident is so reputationally damaging to the family, that the family member in the news is dismissed from their board seat at a non-affiliated publicly traded company. While tragedies cannot always be avoided, had the company properly coordinated their advisors they could have mitigated the damage of this event.*

The questions usually are:

- Did they do everything to avoid the accident?
- Did they have proper insurance coverages in place before it became a lawsuit?
- Did they coordinate and engage with media consultants to mitigate the negative publicity?

---

[2] *United States Supreme Court. "Connelly v. United States." Supreme Court of the United States, 2024, www.supremecourt.gov/opinions/23pdf/23-146_i42j.pdf.*

While hindsight is always 20/20, a holistic approach to risk management would ask the 'what if' questions before an adverse event to ensure proper planning strategies are in place.

Inefficient Resource Allocation

When asset growth and risk management strategies are developed in isolation, families may end up overspending in some areas while leaving others exposed.

For example, *does it make sense for a business owner to invest in a fund made up of companies in the same industry as their own? That decision may concentrate risk rather than diversify it.*

Missed Opportunity to Coordinate

A siloed approach may overlook ways to integrate asset growth and risk management strategies. The exposures associated with a bifurcated risk management strategy increase as a family adds more assets and expands into new Asset Silos

Consider a family *with their primary home in the Midwest and a second home at the beach. They hire two local insurance agents, each with regional expertise but those advisors never speak to each other. The family assumes their golf cart, primarily used in their Midwest gated community is covered appropriately on their homeowner's policy as advised by their agent in the Midwest.*

They wrongfully assume the golf cart is likewise covered for use at the beach house as well. However, local regulations differ, and when their son causes a fatal accident while driving the golf cart on public roads near the beach house, the family discovers they're uninsured. Because of the missed opportunity to coordinate advisors, they're now exposed to a catastrophic lawsuit and financial loss.

The Need for Integrated Risk Management

Figure 1.6 Integrated Risk Management Model: Unified strategy and cross-disciplinary oversight in action.

Holistic wealth and risk management necessitates an Integrated Risk Management approach, a collaborative, structured method that addresses the full spectrum of potential threats. This model would likely include:

- **A Unified Strategy:** A comprehensive plan that accounts for all aspects of a family's financial and personal life, integrating asset growth strategies with proactive risk management measures across all Asset Silos.

- **A Coordinated Professional Collaboration:** Financial advisors, attorneys, insurance experts, tax professionals, and others working collaboratively to achieve a unified vision across all Asset Silos.

- **A Proactive Risk Identification:** Ongoing assessment of financial, legal, reputational, operational, and even personal risk across all Asset Silos.

- **Holistic Risk Management Program:** Multi-layered strategies, like insurance, legal structures, and contingency planning, tailored to the family's unique exposures as related to all Asset Silos.
- **Ongoing Monitoring and Adjustment:** Regular reviews to adapt to the evolving family circumstances, economic trends, and emerging threats. A major loss event can also drive urgent need for adjustment, as the financial, or otherwise strain, on the family may result in a recalculated Risk Tolerance given the new circumstances. In essence, a major hit from Financial Gravity can completely change a family's wealth and risk management strategies.

Publicly traded companies understand this well, many appoint a Chief Risk Officer or establish a risk management committee within their board of directors. Families should do the same.

Below are a few examples of how understanding how Integrated Risk Management can affect long-term success, or failure of a strategy:

Apparel Company's Cotton Sourcing Dilemma

A fast-fashion apparel retailer serving ethically conscious consumers discovers a new supplier offering cotton at 20% less cost. On paper, this appears to be a financial win. But the supplier allegedly uses marginalized people working under unethical conditions as laborers.

A short-term gain may lead to a long-term disaster if it is not managed correctly. Reputational damage could result in lost customers and depressed revenues far exceeding the initial savings. It's the Risk Manager's job to analyze the opportunity as it relates to potential exposure through the lens of the four tools of risk management: **Avoidance, Mitigation, Transference, or Assumption** as they weigh that risk.

Now imagine, the same cotton supplier opportunity but in the context of a rag manufacturer. This rag manufacturer is primarily selling to heavy industry, potentially a far less socially conscious industry. In this case, the ***Reputational Risk*** *is minimal, and the savings might make sense, context* *matters. A qualified Risk Manager can assess the decision within the complete picture of the family's values, assets, and tolerance.*

As we'll explore in future chapters, any decision, whether for asset growth or protection, can trigger unintended consequences in other Asset Silos. Without a framework and team to assess those ripple effects, families remain vulnerable.

That's why a coordinated, cross-disciplinary risk strategy is essential. It ensures families are clearly Informed, fully understanding which risks they are Avoiding, Mitigating, Transferring, or Assuming, and why. Ultimately, it's okay, sometimes necessary, to take calculated risks so long as it's done from a perspective of eyes-wide-open.

Checklist & Key Questions

- Have we evaluated our wealth through an integrated lens, or are our assets and risks still being managed in disconnected silos?
- Which risks are we currently assuming, explicitly or implicitly, without having consciously decided that those risks align with our tolerance and values?
- Are we prioritizing risks based on frequency and severity?
- Do we have clear accountability for risk oversight across all Asset Silos, including off-balance-sheet, reputational, legal, and operational exposures? If not, who is effectively playing, or failing to play, the Risk Manager role?
- Have our advisors been coordinated around a unified strategy, or are key decisions (estate planning, insurance, investments, business operations) being made independently without shared context?
- If a single adverse event occurred tomorrow in one Asset Silo, are we confident we understand the cascading financial, legal, and reputational consequences across the rest of our balance sheet?

Conclusion
The Importance of Managing Risk Through the Total Family Balance Sheet Framework

Holistic wealth and risk management places equal emphasis on both the preservation and growth of wealth. It's about more than just asset accumulation; it's about building a resilient financial foundation that can endure unforeseen challenges and protect family legacy across generations.

By adopting this comprehensive approach, families can better anticipate threats, leverage coordinated strategies, and make Informed decisions. The chapters that follow will explore specific tools and techniques for implementing the Total Family Balance Sheet framework, helping empower families to manage complexity with clarity and confidence in today's evolving financial landscape.

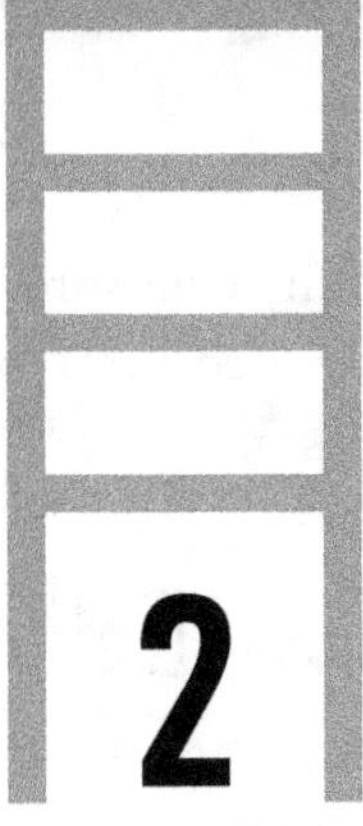

A HOLISTIC VIEW

Introducing the Total Family Balance Sheet Framework

For successful families, the traditional balance sheet offers an incomplete, and often misleading, view of their financial reality. It focuses predominantly on assets and scheduled liabilities, frequently neglecting equally important unaccounted-for or Off-balance-sheet-liabilities and their complex interplay.

Beyond Assets: A Truly Comprehensive Liability Assessment

The Total Family Balance Sheet approach to risk management moves beyond the limitations of traditional financial statements. It recognizes that proper financial security isn't just about asset accumulation, but about strategically mitigating the liabilities that could jeopardize those assets. The framework shifts the focus from a static snapshot of net worth to a dynamic evaluation of both assets and total liabilities and the complex relationships between them.

This chapter introduces the Total Family Balance Sheet risk management framework: a revolutionary tool that systematically assesses and manages a family's unaccounted-for liability exposures across all facets of their life in conjunction with traditionally used tools, offering a truly comprehensive view of their financial well-being.

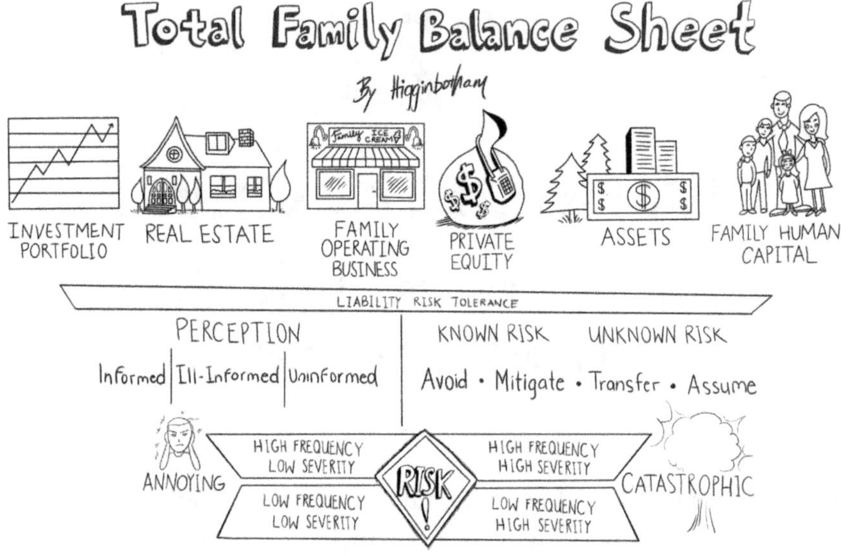

Figure 2.1 The Total Family Balance Sheet in Practice: The Total Family Balance Sheet Framework as a strategic decision-making tool, mapping risk, awareness, and strategy across all silos.

At the top of *The Total Family Balance Sheet by Higginbotham*™ framework sits the family's Asset Silos, representing the full landscape of assets including family human capital. Beneath this foundation, the framework examines the family's Risk Tolerance and risk perception, recognizing what the family knows about the risks and how a family feels about risk.

From there, the framework focuses on identifying both known and unknown risks across all Asset Silos. Once risks are surfaced, the family determines how each should be addressed using the four tools of risk management: Avoidance, Mitigation, Transference, or Assumption.

Finally, the framework evaluates each risk through the lens of frequency and severity of loss, ensuring that decisions are prioritized based on the likelihood of occurrence and the magnitude of potential impact on the family.

Asset Silos

This innovative framework systematically examines a family's risk exposure across six key verticals, or Asset Silos. Regardless of net worth, every family faces potential risks and liabilities, many of which are often overlooked. The six categories are:

1. Investment Portfolios

Includes stocks, bonds, mutual funds, ETFs, currencies, commodities, derivatives, and passive investments in real estate investment trusts, hedge funds, and private equity funds.

2. Real Estate Holdings

Covers actively owned and managed residential, agricultural, raw land, project developments, and commercial properties. If held passively, these may be classified as part of the Investment Portfolio or Private Equity.

3. Family Operating Business

Any business where the family holds significant ownership and manages operations, hiring, culture, and daily decisions.

4. Private Equity Investments

Direct investments or hard money loans into privately held companies. This does not include managed Private Equity funds, but refers to companies where the family has a vested interest.

5. Personal Assets

Valuable possessions like art, vehicles, boats, jet skis, motorcycles, jewelry, and collectibles, as well as primary and secondary residences. Income-generating properties may fall under other asset class categories, like Real Estate.

6. Family Human Capital

Often overlooked, this includes the family's intellectual property, reputation, relationships, influence, and skills, the "brand" that supports deal-making and access to opportunities.

Risk Tolerance

Figure 2.2 Physical & Emotional Risk Tolerance: Liability Risk Tolerance shown as two interdependent components, financial capacity (Physical) and psychological comfort (Emotional), that must align for clear decision-making.

The Total Family Balance Sheet also considers a family's liability Risk Tolerance, which includes:

- **Physical (Financial):** The family's actual ability to absorb losses without compromising their financial security. The more assets a family has, the more risk it can technically absorb.
- **Emotional:** The family's comfort level with those risks. Ironically, families with more wealth often become more risk-averse, choosing to protect rather than leverage their position.

Ultimately, satisfaction with any financial outcome depends on how these two forces, financial capacity and emotional readiness, align.

Understanding Risk Perception: Informed, Ill-Informed, Uninformed

The risks associated with these vertical "asset classes" will be explored in detail in the chapters ahead, along with the concepts related to the four tools of risk management: Avoidance, Mitigation, Transference, or Assumption.

Figure 2.3 Liability Risk Tolerance: *A spectrum showing how families assess and balance their liability risk tolerance through the many factors that drive their risk tolerance which likely change over time.*

With risk, hindsight is always 20/20. Far too often, families and companies believe they have a solid grasp of their exposures, and the impact a loss may have, only to be blindsided by something unexpected.

The process most go through is thinking that they are Informed, only to find out that they were Ill-Informed, which ultimately leads to them being Uninformed.

- **Informed of Risk:** This is what you know. Informed Risk represents a clear understanding of the potential risks, their likelihood, and their potential impact.
- **Ill-Informed of Risk:** What you should know or think you know. This is perhaps the most dangerous category, where assumptions and incomplete information create a false sense of security.

- **Uninformed of Risk:** This is what you don't know. This denotes a complete lack of awareness of potential risks.

These concepts will be explored further in Chapter 4.

Tools of Risk Management: Identify, Avoid, Mitigate, Transfer, or Assume

In risk management, it is essential to distinguish between known risks and unknown risks.

- **Known Risks:** Those risks that are identifiable and measurable.
- **Unknown Risks:** These risks are unpredictable and difficult to quantify, often emerging without warning and beyond the scope of traditional planning. Often, most unknown risks are indefinable through a coordinated approach and proper planning.

Effective risk management requires addressing both categories, and choosing to actively manage the risks through Avoidance, Mitigation, Transference, or Assumption.

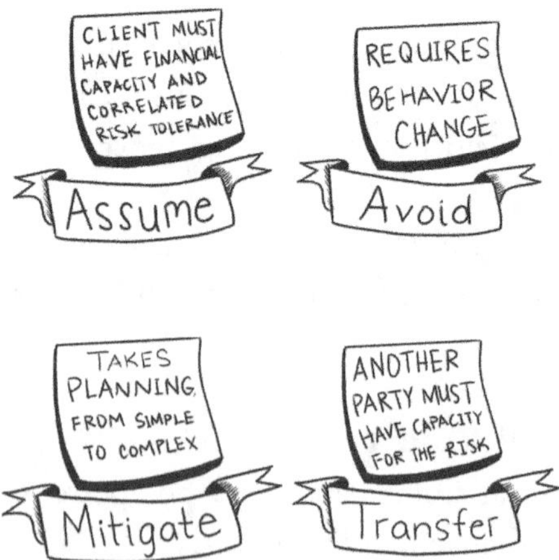

Figure 2.4 Strategic Approaches: The four foundational risk strategies, Avoid, Mitigate, Transfer, or Assume, used in tandem based on likelihood, severity, and tolerance.

Once risk exposure and awareness levels are assessed, the framework evaluates four strategic responses:

1. **Avoid** – Avoidance removes the risk entirely, typically requiring a change in behavior or decisions such as exiting a risky investment or opting not to enter a legal agreement.
2. **Mitigate** – Mitigation reduces the likelihood or impact of a risk and often involves proactive planning. This can range from maintenance and safety upgrades to diversification strategies.
3. **Transfer** –Transference shifts the financial burden through selling the risk to a third party, usually through insurance, contracts, or legal structures. The other party must have the capacity to assume the risk being transferred.
4. **Assume** – Assumption is when a family has both the financial means and the emotional tolerance to accept a risk, they may choose to assume it. This is most effective when exposure is well understood and strategically planned.

Loss Frequency and Severity

The relationship between loss frequency and loss severity is central to understanding risk dynamics. Losses can be categorized across four quadrants: low frequency/low severity, low frequency/high severity, high frequency/low severity, and high frequency/high severity. Each quadrant reflects a distinct risk profile, influencing how organizations prioritize and allocate resources for protection. By recognizing where a potential exposure falls within this framework, decision-makers can better tailor risk management strategies to balance efficiency with resilience.

These concepts and tools will be discussed in the following chapters in greater detail.

Checklist & Key Questions

- Are we evaluating risks holistically across all Asset Silos, rather than addressing them in isolation?
- Have we accounted for any off-balance-sheet exposures, legal, operational, reputational, or otherwise, that may impact our overall risk posture?
- Do our financial (physical) and Emotional Risk Tolerances align to support clear decision-making?
- Are we truly Informed about our risks, or are we relying on assumptions that leave us Ill-Informed or unaware?
- Have we intentionally determined whether we will avoid, mitigate, transfer, or assume our major risks, and do we have structured plans in place with full awareness of the implications of each choice?
- Do we understand the frequency and severity of each potential loss so we can prioritize our planning effectively?
- Are the family's advisors communicating and coordinating to prevent blind spots, overlaps, or gaps in our risk strategy?
- Do we have a clearly defined Risk Manager role responsible for cross-silo oversight and integrated decision-making?
- Are we unintentionally over-preparing for lower probability risks while overlooking higher probability threats?
- Have we assessed how risks in one silo may cascade into others, creating compounding or correlated vulnerabilities?
- Are we proactively identifying emerging risks and adjusting our strategies when the family's circumstances or external conditions change?

Conclusion
The Ultimate Success: A More Secure Financial Future

The Total Family Balance Sheet reframes how successful families understand and manage their wealth by shifting the focus from a static snapshot of assets to a dynamic, holistic evaluation of risk across all areas of life.

By identifying exposures within each of the six Asset Silos, uncovering Off-balance-sheet-liabilities, assessing both **Physical** and **Emotional Risk Tolerance**, and applying the appropriate risk management tools, families gain clarity on vulnerabilities that traditional planning often overlooks.

This framework empowers families to move beyond assumptions and fragmented decision-making toward coordinated, proactive strategies that reduce blind spots, prevent cross-silo contagion, and ensure every major risk is intentionally Avoided, Mitigated, Transferred, or Assumed. Families who adopt this approach often find that their risk management strategies become more efficient and cost-effective, their protection from financial, legal, operational, and reputational threats becomes stronger, and their exposure to catastrophic Financial Gravity events is significantly reduced. They also benefit from greater alignment among advisors and a more accurate, transparent understanding of their true net-worth resilience.

Ultimately, the Total Family Balance Sheet is more than a diagnostic tool: it is a roadmap for long-term continuity, stability, and confidence. By integrating its principles into their ongoing planning, families build not only a clearer financial picture but also a more durable foundation capable of sustaining their wealth and legacy for generations to come.

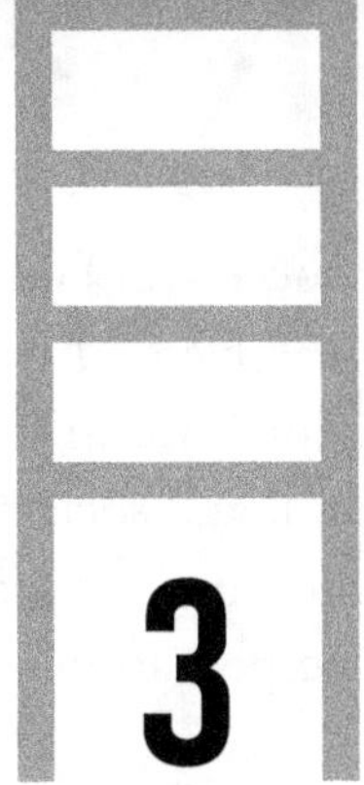

3

THE PERFECT STORM

Why Managing Risk Matters Now More Than Ever

Figure 3.1 Always Shifting Financial Landscape: Interest rate whiplash, asset repricing, and liquidity risk: how today's market environment challenges traditional risk assumptions.

The world has changed. For successful families, the traditional approach to risk management, often reactive and fragmented, is no longer sufficient. We stand at a unique juncture in history, where a confluence of macroeconomic, environmental, and societal factors has created a perfect storm, demanding a comprehensive, proactive, and holistic approach to risk management for wealth perpetuation.

Macroeconomic Instability: A Shifting Financial Landscape

A decade or more of historically low interest rates, followed by the recent rapid surge in interest rates, has profoundly reshaped the financial landscape. This rapid increase, coupled with already-existing economic uncertainties and increasing economic impact of environmental disasters, has exposed vulnerabilities within our financial system. Less financially solvent insurance companies, banks, and financial institutions, burdened by increased liabilities, reduced investment returns, and a need to liquidate their bond portfolios at a discount to meet their liabilities, reducing many institutions' financial strength and forcing many rating agencies (i.e. Moody's and AM Best) to adjust the financial rating of those institutions downward.

This instability has significant implications for families who have needed to liquidate their portfolios and those relying on insurance for protection against various risks. If your insurance provider is downgraded or is forced into insolvency by a regulator, your policy's value in a worst-case scenario could be worthless or significantly diminished as you are now forced to rely on the limited protection of a given state's insurance guarantee fund. This can leave you and your family exposed and potentially without the critical coverage you thought you had secured. Just like the Federal Government provides FDIC insurance for banks to cover your deposited funds with a limit of up to $250,000, insurance is regulated by the states, which have put guarantee programs in place to backstop and protect families and companies from an insolvent insurance carrier. These limits vary by state, policy type and are often updated. In 2024, the limit in New York State was the highest at \$500,000 for a life insurance policy, whereas the lowest was in California at \$80,000 for a long-term care insurance policy.[3] This highlights the importance of choosing financial institutions and insurance carriers with a strong financial rating.

Correlation of Frequency and Severity

The frequency and severity of extreme events are escalating at an alarming rate. Between 2023 and 2024, the United States experienced 55 disasters, resulting in over \$275 billion in damages and losses.[4] This figure dwarfs the 30-year average of only eight such events annually. Regardless of the cause of environmental catastrophes, the financial impact is driven by population and migration patterns, which tend to aggregate assets in each area; many areas are naturally more susceptible to these events.

For example, the significant population increase in South Florida over the last 50 years, combined with the value of the assets now present there (i.e., homes, commercial real estate, electrical infrastructure, etc.), leads to escalating costs associated with these events. Homes, businesses, and entire communities are increasingly vulnerable to flooding, wildfires, thunderstorms, hurricanes, and other extreme weather phenomena. The financial implications of such events are staggering, often exceeding the capacity of many traditional insurance models.

---

[3] *"Financial Stability and the Department of Financial Services." New York State Department of Financial Services, www.dfs.ny.gov/consumers/health_insurance/financial_stability_and_the_department_of_financial_services.*
[4] *NOAA National Centers for Environmental Information. "U.S. Billion-Dollar Weather and Climate Disasters." NCEI, 2025, www.ncei.noaa.gov/access/billions/. DOI: 10.25921/stkw-7w73.*

Social Inflation: The Rise of Litigation and Erosion of Trust

Figure 3.2 Rise of Litigation and Social Inflation: An upward trend in legal verdicts, litigation funding, and societal distrust, driving higher risk and higher premiums for individuals and businesses.

Beyond the macroeconomic and environmental pressures, a surge in **Social Inflation** further complicates the risk landscape. This isn't simply about rising costs; it's a fundamental shift in the legal and societal environment:

- **Nuclear Legal Verdicts:** The volume of jury awards exceeding $10 million have surged to unprecedented levels in recent years, reshaping the litigation landscape for individuals' families and corporations. According to the 2025 Nuclear Verdicts Report by Marathon Strategies, 135 corporate lawsuits resulted in nuclear verdicts in 2024, the highest number identified since record keeping began in 2009, with total awards reaching approximately $31.3 billion. The median nuclear verdict climbed to $51 million in 2024, up from $44 million in 2023, but even more striking is the rise compared to the early pandemic era, when the median hovered around $21 million in 2020, a level that reflected a temporary dip in litigation activity as courts closed and filings slowed.[5] The sharp increase in both the frequency and size of these verdicts illustrates how societal, legal, and economic forces have combined to accelerate "nuclear" outcomes well beyond pre-pandemic norms, exposing companies to greater financial and reputational risk than ever before.

- **Erosion of Trust:** Growing distrust in government bodies, large corporations, and institutions has emboldened those seeking to leverage legal avenues to achieve financial consequences against their adversaries.

- **Private Equity's Role:** Additionally, there is a financial commercialization of the plaintiff's legal system, where private equity has moved into funding torts, creating a new industry known as **Litigation Finance.** Most will not have to look far on any major highway in the United States to see the billboards that highlight the influx of capital spent on advertising in this space.

- **Regulatory Considerations:** The constant change in regulations, combined with the difficulty in interpreting and adhering to them, as well as a challenging enforcement landscape, increases the likelihood of compliance failures and subsequent penalties. Many times, the lack of compliance is not nefarious; it's simply a result of regulatory complexity.

These trends collectively increase the likelihood of more litigation on more fronts, and with higher stakes. From a risk management perspective, the result increases the cost of virtually all aspects of business, from insurance premiums to compliance audits, as well as printing warning labels on plastic bags stating that they are 'not a toy suitable for kids.'

Rising Interest Rates - A decade of near-zero short-term bond rates forced many people and/or institutions who need to hold cash reserve positions, either driven by regulatory rules or portfolio management, to go long in their bond position to get some rate of return. These individuals and

---

[5] Marathon Strategies, Corporate Verdicts Go Thermonuclear: Nuclear Verdicts Report 2025 (May 2025), https://marathonstrategies.com/wp-content/uploads/2025/05/Nuclear-Verdicts-Report-2025.pdf

institutions have faced difficulties selling their low-yield bonds at a discount to cover inflationary costs. For nearly a decade, they could sell those bonds for the same price they had paid for them. Overnight, they found themselves in a situation where, if they needed cash, they would have to take a loss on the sale of those bonds.

Bank Failure in Silicon Valley

Anyone who has experienced a significant cash call knows the strain that sudden, unexpected liquidity demands can place on a family's or a business's financial structure. For example, a well-known California bank failed largely because of a mismatch between the duration of its bond portfolio and its short-term liquidity needs. The bank invested heavily in long-term government and mortgage-backed securities when interest rates were low, locking up large portions of its balance sheet in assets highly sensitive to rate increases. When interest rates rose sharply, the value of those bonds dropped, creating significant unrealized losses. At the same time, depositors, many of them venture-backed companies, began drawing down cash, forcing this bank to sell portions of its bond portfolio at a steep loss to meet liquidity demands. This sale not only crystallized the losses but also spooked depositors, accelerating the run on the bank and ultimately leading to its collapse. Further, it is said that more than 85% of the bank's deposits exceeded the FDIC insurance limit of $250,000.[6] Ultimately, the government stepped in and guaranteed the deposits in full, which may not always be the case.

Florida Insurance Carrier Insolvency

Over the past five years, over 20 Florida domiciled insurance carriers serving the Gulf Coast have failed. Many of which were undone by the same bond portfolio pressures that crippled larger financial institutions.[7] As interest rates climbed, the long duration bonds these insurers held lost significant value, eroding their capital reserves and leaving them unable to meet mounting claims, causing a situation akin to a 'run on the bank'. The insurance carriers needed the cash to pay claims, at a time when the value of their

---

[6] *"Silicon Valley Bank Deposit Insurance." Time, www.time.com/6262009/silicon-valley-bank-deposit-insurance/.*

[7] *"Insolvency Reports." Florida Department of Financial Services, Division of Receiver, myfloridacfo.com/division/receiver/companies/insolvency-reports.*

bond portfolio was likely worth materially less than what it had been. These failures, and potentially those to come, are particularly true in states vulnerable to high-cost catastrophes. The larger, more financially solvent insurance carriers often will pull out of those higher-risk environments creating a cottage industry for smaller, more risk-tolerant insurance carriers who cannot weather the storm with the same capacity. When these carriers fail, policyholders are forced to rely on the state guaranty association for coverage, which often provides materially less protection than the original policies promised. This can leave many homeowners and businesses exposed, with coverage limits falling short of their true risk transfer needs, underscoring the macroeconomic factors that expose insurance carriers (and other financial institutions) to vulnerabilities.

In both cases, it's not to say financial institutions don't have merit; it's to highlight the importance of a comprehensive, coordinated, and monitored approach to risk management.

Checklist & Key Questions

- What major risks are we currently assuming knowingly or not?
- Have we evaluated the financial strength of the institutions we put our trust in?
- Have we evaluated each Asset Silo for known and unknown risks with coordinated oversight?
- Do we have a Risk Manager role defined in our advisor network?
- Are we focusing on the most probable risks or the most visible ones?
- How well do our risk strategies align with our Risk Tolerance?

Conclusion
Managing Changing Times Using the Total Family Balance Sheet Framework

The world has changed. For successful families, a reactive and fragmented approach to risk management is no longer enough. Macroeconomic instability, environmental disruption, and social inflation are converging in ways that make risk more frequent, more severe, and more interconnected than ever before.

What makes today's environment especially dangerous is that risk rarely stays contained. A breakdown in one area can quickly spill into others. Liquidity stress can pressure investment portfolios. Litigation can threaten operating entities, personal assets, and reputation. A catastrophe event can expose coverage gaps and carrier weakness at the exact moment protection is needed most. Risk moves across silos, even when families manage them separately.

That is the vulnerability. Risk is integrated, but management often is not.

The solution is not to avoid risk, but to manage it with structure and discipline. Families need clear governance, coordinated oversight, and someone accountable for seeing the full picture across the total family balance sheet. The families who thrive in this era will be the ones who identify interdependencies early, act before issues compound, and build resilience into their system.

The Total Family Balance Sheet framework provides that structure. It is a practical way to connect the silos, clarify accountability, and create a repeatable process for protecting what matters most. In a world where the stakes are higher and the margin for error is smaller, comprehensive risk management is no longer optional. It is essential to wealth perpetuation.

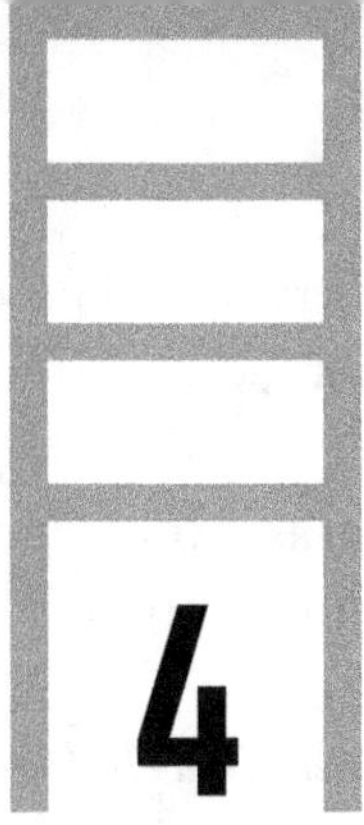

CHARTING THE COURSE
Understanding Risk and Risk Tolerance

Risk. It's a word that whispers uneasily in boardrooms and board games alike. For the ultra-high net worth individual or family, however, understanding and managing risk transcends the theoretical; it's a crucial determinant of legacy and financial well-being. This chapter explores the multifaceted nature of risk, examining its various forms and delving into the essential concept of Risk Tolerance.

The Many Faces of Risk

Risk isn't a monolithic entity. It manifests in diverse forms, each demanding a unique approach to assumptions and fragmented decision-making toward coordinated, proactive strategies that reduce blind spots, prevent cross-silo contagion, and ensure every major risk is intentionally avoided, mitigated, transferred, or assumed. Let's examine a few key categories, which are generally intertwined:

Financial Risk: This encompasses the potential for loss of capital due to market fluctuations, poor investments, or unforeseen economic downturns, as well as downward pressure on net worth accumulation from external factors like property or casualty loss.

Reputational Risk: This refers to the potential harm to an individual, family, or business due to actions, events, and associations that can damage stakeholder and societal trust. In today's hyper-connected world, damage to one's reputation can be devastating and result in significant financial loss. It is featured in our headlines often.

Consider an iconic bank that is well known for their legacy of moving gold across the American West in stagecoaches. Their reputation was built on one of legacy and trust, leaving many of today's consumers and businesses to intrinsically trust their operating procedures. When the headlines hit that this 'trusted' institution had retail-level bank tellers, who were facetiously creating bank accounts for unaware banking customers, its reputation suffered.

This situation caused significant long-term reputational damage, reduction of stakeholder trust, and financial harm to an iconic brand. Reputational Risk and its potential economic consequences are not unique to multi-national, billion-dollar brands; on a varying scale, this risk can impact anyone, from individuals and families to small business owners and institutions like school districts and universities.

Operational Risk: This category encompasses disruptions caused by internal failures or external events impacting the day-to-day operations of a business or family office.

Imagine, an international cybersecurity company deploys an update to its software without thoroughly vetting its viability, causing hundreds of millions of terminals to go down and leading to days of productivity disruption for its customers. Ultimately, this results in loss of income claims against the cybersecurity company.

Legal Risk: This term refers to the potential for financial loss, reputational damage, or operational disruption resulting from non-compliance with laws, regulatory breaches, contractual failures, fiduciary breaches, or legal disputes.

Take a national home improvement store who suffered a large-scale data breach, resulting in legal action that led to hundreds of millions of dollars in settlement costs, as well as immeasurable financial losses due to a reduction in consumer confidence.

Strategic Risk: This is the outlier in the group, which is often independent of the other categories of risk. **Strategic Risk** involves the risks present to families or companies as they innovate and make strategic decisions related to new markets, products, services, and so on, that don't materialize as intended.

Figure 4.1 Strategic Risk Misalignment: A failed product launch or market entry, even by a major institution, demonstrates the real-world cost of unchecked strategic assumptions.

Take, for example*, a large auto manufacturer based in Detroit, MI, which made a strategic decision to electrify its best-selling pickup truck, deploying billions of dollars in R&D, infrastructure, and marketing costs, only to be left with a product deemed undesirable by consumers. Many analysts predict that it could take this auto manufacturer a decade or more to recoup its investment in electric vehicles, due to high initial costs and slow adoption rates.*

Risk Perception: What You Know, What You Should Know (or Think You Know), and What You Don't Know

Our ability to assess and manage risk is intrinsically linked to our understanding of it. This understanding falls into three distinct categories:

- **Informed of Risk:** This is what you know. Informed Risk represents a clear understanding of the potential risks, their likelihood, and their potential impact.
- **Ill-Informed of Risk:** What you should know or think you know. This is perhaps the most dangerous category, where assumptions and incomplete information create a false sense of security.
- **Uninformed of Risk:** This is what you don't know. This denotes a complete lack of awareness of potential risks.

Understanding risk often traverses all three categories, as we are usually never as Informed as we think we are.

A good articulation of this in residential property risk is a situation where a thunderstorm results in significant rainfall, causing the flashing connecting your roof to the vertical areas of your chimney to leak. This results in ½ inch of water on the floor of your living room. Your sheet rock is ruined, your carpet is wet, and the water has wicked up into your furniture.

Thinking that you were adequately Informed when you purchased your homeowner's insurance policy, you turn in a claim, believing, "My insurance will cover this damage." The insurance claims adjuster educates you on the contractual language contained within your insurance policy, where it outlines explicitly the 'perils' your home is insured against. Leading you to understand that you were Ill-Informed, as rain through a faulty roof is not a covered 'peril' on your current policy. The claims adjuster goes on to add insult to injury, advising that you could have been covered had you purchased an 'all-risk' policy that would provide coverage for the peril of rain through a faulty roof. You now realize you were completely Uninformed. The adjuster laughingly *goes on to explain that a construction defect caused the source of the leak, as your builder failed to add a 'cricket' between the roof and chimney. While the adoption of an **All-Risk** policy would have provided coverage for the damage to your house and the replacement of your carpet and furniture, it would not have covered the roof repair, as construction defects are typically never covered by insurance policies. Understandably, most people are furious when this situation plays out. The potential permutations of what is, and what is not, covered in this example, in many cases, are just as confusing as the insurance contract language itself.*

Had this family been holistically Informed, the correct insurance could have been in place before the event, or potentially avoided the event entirely had the cricket been installed at the time of the property's construction or acquisition.

With all of this said, it requires a mindset shift relating to managing risk. Families and their advisors must make a paradigm shift from assuming they are Informed to always beginning from a position of being Uninformed, ensuring that their risk is thoroughly evaluated and explained. Leveraging the four tools of risk management (Avoidance, Mitigation, Transference, or Assumption). Specifically, with risk transfer, most insurance is purchased based on the cover page, which provides a summary of coverages, rather than assessing the nuanced contract language (or 'fine print') of the policy itself. By not doing so, a situation is created where everyone is Uninformed and ultimately unsatisfied when a claim arises.

Just like a dentist or a doctor at a cocktail party, Risk Managers are often approached with a current situation related to a risk exposure someone is experiencing. Many times, the inquirer is trying to find coverage, someone to blame, or just a deeper understanding of why the loss is falling to them. As discussed earlier, risk perception is often the driver behind a 'surprise' impact of a risk coming to fruition. Frequently, the person suffering is looking for insurance to respond and is met with a response from the Risk Manager that 'you got exactly what you paid for. Insurance does precisely what the contract says, nothing more, nothing less.'

Figure 4.2 Understanding Risk Tolerance: Visualizing the intersection of emotional and Financial Risk capacity, and why misalignment leads to stalled decision-making or regret.

Was this person Informed, Ill-Informed, and/or Uninformed of this specific risk? Only with a completely Informed knowledge of their exposures as well as a healthy balance between their emotional and **Physical Risk Tolerance** will ultimately deliver satisfaction when it comes to experiencing a loss or the impact of Financial Gravity.

This truly highlights the importance of individuals, families, business owners, professional Risk Managers, and advisors having accurate information before deciding what to do with a specific risk, to purchase an insurance policy or sign a legal agreement, etc.

Risk Tolerance: A Personal Equation

Risk Tolerance isn't a fixed concept; it's defined by personal characteristics influenced by individual circumstances, financial security, and psychological factors. Different individuals, families, and businesses demonstrate varying levels of Risk Tolerance at varying stages. As previously discussed, the concept of Risk Tolerance has to be balanced, monitored and adjusted accordingly to align with emotional and physical needs. The idea of emotional and Physical Risk Tolerance is driven by the three natural tendencies as outlined below.

Figure 4.3 Risk Tolerance Spectrum: At varying stages of life, asset size, needs, etc., one's approach to Risk Tolerance will change over time.

- **Risk-Averse:** This approach prioritizes capital preservation and tends to be more conservative with the adoption or taking of risk, even if it means foregoing potential higher returns or greater reward.
- **Risk-Neutral:** Characterized by those who are willing to accept some risk for the potential of higher returns but strive to maintain a balance between risk and reward.
- **Risk-Seeking:** These individuals embrace risk for the potential of substantial gains, often willing to accept significant losses for the possibility of greater rewards.

Ultimately, an individual, family or business needs to be aware in each facet of life where their Risk Tolerance lies for proper risk management.

For example, a fresh college graduate is involved in a startup technology venture. They think they don't have any meaningful financial net worth; thus, they cannot lose much and take significant risks. Without knowing it they are exposed to potential liability for lawsuits or judgments potentially related to patent infringements or Operational Risks, let alone the risk to their "human capital" or Reputational Risk that can last a lifetime.

Whereas a successful, seasoned veteran can financially absorb more of the financial loss potential associated with the risks present in a startup venture, they are less willing to subject themselves to the known and unaccounted-for liability related to potential punitive legal action or damage to their family reputation. In many cases they will choose not to take the risk, unless they deem the reward is worthy of such risk. From the outside, this can be perceived as 'analysis paralysis', where the veteran takes a more considered approach to their liability Risk Tolerance, and their decision is more heavily weighted toward their Emotional Risk vs. their Physical Risk Tolerance.

The above is a rational consideration related to Physical versus Emotional Risk Tolerance, while also considering one's stance on being **Risk-Averse**, **Risk-Neutral**, or **Risk-Seeking**. On the other hand, many people miss the opportunity to invest or make mistakes in how they manage their risk because their Emotional Risk Tolerance has not grown at the same rate as their Physical Risk Tolerance, while also not balancing the spectrum on their risk appetite scale from Risk-Averse to Risk-Seeking.

Ultimately, the success of managing these variables is what will lead to a family's satisfaction with their overall wealth and risk management strategy. This highlights the importance of having honest and candid vulnerable conversations with a trusted Risk Manager who regularly helps balance these two variables and your risk appetite for Informed decision-making. It is also imperative that anyone impacted by the decision be included in these conversations (spouses, parents, children, beneficiaries, business partners, etc.), as they will all judge the outcome of a given decision with 20/20 hindsight.

Regardless of whether a family takes a given risk, or avoids it, it's imperative the family enter into all decisions with their eyes wide open.

All of this is a tremendous amount to consider, even within one asset class. When layered and coordinated across the six Asset Silos of the Total Family Balance Sheet, and considering the individual advisors working in each silo, multiple family members and/or business partners, as well as a constantly changing landscape, you have the fundamental reason why a comprehensive, coordinated approach to risk management is so critical.

Checklist & Key Questions

- Are we fully Informed about all risk we are exposed to?
- Have we adequately evaluated our Risk Tolerance related to those risks?
- Have we recently assessed our emotional versus physical risk capacity?
- Are we assuming risk we don't fully understand?
- Where do we rely on summary insurance coverage vs. the actual contract?
- When was the last time we reassessed our risk appetite across our family and ventures?
- Are key decision-makers aligned in their perceptions of risk?

Conclusion
Assessing Risk and Risk Tolerance Using the Total Family Balance Sheet

In the end, understanding risk and Risk Tolerance is less about eliminating uncertainty and more about approaching it with clarity, alignment, and discipline. For families and individuals managing wealth, the balance between emotional comfort and financial capacity defines how effectively risks are identified, measured, and addressed. By recognizing the many faces of risk, questioning assumptions about what is known or unknown, and honestly assessing Risk Tolerance, families can make decisions with eyes wide open. This awareness not only supports stronger financial outcomes but also preserves peace of mind, ensuring that wealth serves its intended purpose across generations.

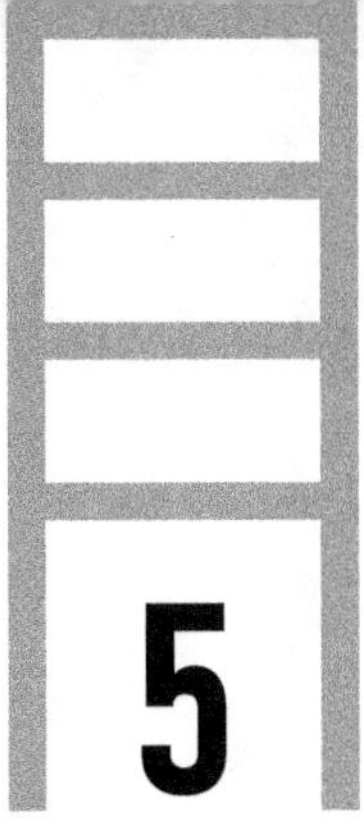

MASTERING RISK

A Deep Dive into the Four Tools of Risk Management

The Total Family Balance Sheet framework isn't simply about identifying risks; it's about strategically managing them. This chapter explores the four tools used for risk management strategies: Avoidance, Mitigation, Transference, and Assumption, examining when each is most suitable and illustrating their application with practical examples.

These four approaches to risk management apply across all Asset Silos of the Total Family Balance Sheet. Families must have a complete understanding of a potential risk, from the perspectives of their knowledge base, 'Informed,' 'Ill-Informed,' or 'Uninformed,' as well as their Emotional and Physical Risk Tolerance to properly implement these risk management approaches initially introduced in Chapter 4. For a family to determine if and to what degree they will implement Avoidance, Mitigation, Transference, or Assumption to any given risk meaningfully and successfully hinges on their level of knowledge about that risk and what can be done with it. Thus, being 'Informed,' 'Ill-Informed,' or 'Uninformed' is the single core driver of when and how to adopt each of the risk management techniques based on your Risk Tolerance. In essence, each risk present in all the silos within the Total Family Balance Sheet Framework requires a family to have proper knowledge of a given risk and which of the four tools of risk management to implement, individually or in combination.

Four Tools of Risk Management

Figure 5.1 Strategic Risk Approaches Explained: *A decision matrix for choosing the right strategy, or mix, for any risk scenario, calibrated to your family's tolerance.*

1. Avoidance: Eliminating Risk Exposure

Remove the risk entirely but recognize when it's realistic to do so.

Avoidance involves proactively eliminating or reducing exposure to a specific risk. This is the most effective strategy when the potential negative consequences of a risk significantly outweigh its potential benefits. Avoidance is often the optimal solution from a risk management perspective, as it removes the risk entirely; however, in many cases, doing so is neither practical nor executable. In its purest form, Avoidance cannot be fully executed in the course of everyday life.

For instance, a company might avoid entering a new, highly volatile market to prevent potential substantial losses, or avoid a specific product line due to significant legal liability exposure. However, risk Avoidance isn't always practical or feasible. Altogether, avoiding all risks, even low-probability ones, would severely restrict an organization's ability to operate and grow.

A business cannot reasonably prevent all market fluctuations or technological disruptions; instead, it employs strategies to assume, mitigate, or transfer those risks. The decision to avoid a risk should be made after careful consideration of its potential severity versus the possible limitations on the business if that risk is avoided. One key challenge with Risk Avoidance is that it often requires a significant change in established behavior, typically starting at the top of an organization, which is then hopefully driven down to the individual behaviors of all team members.

For example, a family with a low Risk Tolerance might avoid investing in highly volatile emerging markets, opting instead for more conservative investments despite potentially lower returns. This approach avoids the risk of substantial capital losses. The best families would have a Family Financial Governance strategy that states this as part of their investment mandate.

As discussed in Chapter 12, Family Human Capital, merely having the structure and documentation is not enough; the family needs assurances that the mandates are being followed so that their risk avoidance strategy is adhered to.

The reality is that risk avoidance becomes difficult when it requires a change in personal behavior. Time and again, we see high-profile individuals face preventable consequences from poor decisions, particularly in situations involving alcohol, late-night events, and impaired judgment. In many of these cases, the issue is not the consumption itself, but the decision to continue operating as if nothing has changed. The consequence could often be avoided through a simple behavioral shift, such as choosing not to drive and instead relying on a car service, a driver, or a trusted alternative plan.

Take a famous actor who is frequently in the tabloids for driving while intoxicated. Some of the behavior changes they could consider avoiding a DWI are as follows:

- Don't partake in the substance(s).
- Don't drive while partaking.
- Partake and wait an adequate amount of time to return to sobriety before driving.

- Hire a car service, while under the influence.
- Hire a driver or designate a sober driver while under the influence.

Implementing these Avoidance strategies may be challenging for the actor for several reasons, including the self-awareness required to recognize when they have been overserved, as well as the necessary discipline and humility to act on it.

Even if the actor meaningfully avoided the risks of his behavior, he could still be subject to a fatal DWI-related incident from another driver.

There are numerous solutions to mitigating risk through Avoidance. The point is that changing behavior is challenging, and risk persists even when implementing avoidance strategies.

From a Total Family Balance Sheet Framework perspective, risk avoidance transcends all Asset Silos and, in many cases, impossible to avoid entirely. To highlight that point, here is a simple example:

In 1984, a known Governor went for a jog before work one day, and a tree limb fell off a sizeable oak tree, landing on him and crushing his spine, leaving him permanently disabled. With that said, total Risk Avoidance is often very difficult to implement because it requires a change in established behavior and discipline to make it happen; even with these changes, risk is always present around everyone.

Ultimately, while Avoidance can sometimes reduce exposure to specific threats, it cannot serve as a universal solution. Risk is inherent in life, business, and wealth management, and even the most carefully designed Avoidance strategies cannot eliminate every possibility of loss. Attempting to sidestep all risks would not only be impractical but would also limit growth, opportunity, and innovation. The more effective approach is to recognize that risk is ever-present and unavoidable, and to focus on building structures and strategies that balance Avoidance with Assumption, Mitigation, and Transference, ensuring resilience in the face of the unexpected.

2. Mitigation: Reducing the Likelihood or Impact of Risk

Plan for the hit of Financial Gravity, so when it comes, you can absorb it.

Mitigation involves implementing measures to reduce either the likelihood or the severity of a potential loss. This strategy is appropriate when the risk can't be entirely avoided but can be managed to reduce its negative impact.

Risk Mitigation is a cornerstone of effective risk management, focusing on reducing the likelihood or impact of an identified risk. Unlike Avoidance, which eliminates the risk, mitigation seeks to lessen its potential consequences. This strategy is frequently applied across various scenarios.

For example, *implementing robust cybersecurity measures to reduce the impact of a data breach, diversifying investments to lessen market volatility, or implementing safety protocols to minimize workplace accidents. Mitigation makes sense when the risk cannot be entirely avoided. Still, its negative impacts can be lessened to an acceptable level, offering a balance between risk reduction and operational efficiency. However, mitigation may not be the most appropriate strategy for low-probability, low-severity risks, where the cost of implementing mitigation measures may exceed the potential loss; in such instances, risk assumption might be more practical. The suitability of mitigation depends on a comprehensive cost-benefit analysis and a clear understanding of the individuals, families, or organization's Risk Tolerance.*

A family living in an earthquake-prone region might mitigate the risk of property damage by retrofitting their home to meet up-to-date seismic building codes. This reduces the likelihood of damage from a more minor earthquake and hopefully offsets, 'mitigates', losses and damage incurred from any seismic activity.

Furthermore, the devastation of Hurricane Ike on Bolivar Peninsula in 2008 served as a stark reminder of the power of nature, and the importance of risk mitigation in coastal construction. While much of the area was leveled by the storm's brutal winds and surge, a handful of homes stood defiantly against the destruction, and their survival is a testament to modern building codes and forward-thinking design. Elevated high above storm surge levels, these structures were anchored with reinforced pilings, hurricane clips, and impact-resistant materials, ensuring they could withstand winds exceeding 130 mph. Their breakaway walls allowed floodwaters to pass through without compromising structural integrity, while fortified roofs and storm shutters protected against flying debris. These homes embodied the principles of risk mitigation, proactive measures that, though costly upfront, safeguarded lives and property when catastrophe struck. In a world where extreme weather is becoming increasingly frequent, their survival underscores a crucial truth: resilience is not just built in response to disaster, but in anticipation and through actions taken to mitigate risk.

From a Total Family Balance Sheet Framework perspective, risk mitigation is essential across all aspects of family planning.

Consider a family *with a low-Risk Tolerance who decides to implement a higher up-front cost approach to healthcare, including a comprehensive wellness program with regular health and fitness assessments, rather than relying solely on emergency healthcare services. This choice potentially reduces the risk of unexpected medical expenses and better ensures the family's well-being. The most effective families establish a detailed Family Health Governance strategy that explicitly outlines their approach to managing health-related risks. As discussed in Chapter 12, Family Human Capital, having the right structures and documentation is not sufficient on its own; the family must ensure that these health guidelines and preventive measures are consistently followed. This involves regular assessments and oversight to confirm that all members adhere to the agreed-upon health practices, thereby protecting their overall quality of life and helping to prevent crises. This is a prime example of how mitigation in one specific area can transcend all silos of the Total Family Balance Sheet framework.*

To further make the point: how often will we hear a successful person say something like 'I would not be able to achieve at this level of success, if I didn't have my health.' The point is that if they are truly taking this opportunity seriously and doing so consistently, their health is a foundational element that helps enable them to continue building across all aspects of personal and professional growth. The caveat to this is that if we ask that successful person, 'What are your health numbers (i.e., A1C, resting heart rate, etc.)?' they may likely respond, 'I don't know, I haven't had a checkup for years'.

3. Transference: Shifting Risk to a Third Party

Shift the burden, but only if the terms, costs, and conditions are clearly understood.

Transference involves shifting all, or a portion, of risk to a third party, typically through insurance policies, other indemnity clauses, or contractual agreements, as well as other risk financing mechanisms, such as captive insurance strategies. Risk Transfer is particularly effective when the potential financial impact of a risk is substantial, and the family has sufficient resources to cover the cost of transferring the risk (i.e., insurance premiums).

As a key strategy in risk management, transfer shifts the burden of potential losses associated with a specific risk to a third party. This is most frequently achieved through insurance policies, where the insurer assumes the financial responsibility for covered losses in exchange for premiums. Typical applications include purchasing liability insurance to protect against lawsuits, property insurance to cover damage to assets, and health insurance to manage healthcare costs. Transfer makes excellent sense for high-severity, low-probability risks where the potential loss significantly outweighs the cost of transferring the risk to an insurer or third party.

Figure 5.2 Strategic Overlap Between Mitigation and Transfer:
Illustrates how proactive risk mitigation strategies and formal risk transfer tools (like insurance or indemnity) can complement one another, especially when complete Avoidance is unrealistic.

When you pay an insurance premium, you are essentially selling your risk to a third party. Instead of carrying the full financial burden of potential loss yourself, you transfer that responsibility to the insurance carrier in exchange for a set price. The carrier "buys" your risk by agreeing to assume the financial consequences of covered events, while you "sell" it by relinquishing the uncertainty and volatility that could otherwise impact your balance sheet. In this way, premiums are not just an expense, they are the cost of converting unpredictable risk into contractual certainty.

When transferring risk to a third-party insurance carrier, careful evaluation of the carrier itself is just as important as the coverage being purchased. Key selection criteria include the carrier's capacity for the risk, ensuring they have the financial strength to absorb large or complex exposures, and the scope of coverage, verifying that the policy language aligns with the actual risks at hand. Decision-makers should also weigh whether the carrier is a stock or mutual company, as this impacts how profits and obligations are prioritized, and consider whether the carrier is admitted or non-admitted, which determines regulatory oversight and access to guaranty funds. The carrier's financial rating provides confidence in long-term solvency, while their claims handling history reflects how they will perform when protection is most needed. Beyond technical criteria, factors like ease of doing business, the quality of the brokers you choose to do business with and the strength of their relationship with the carrier, and ultimately, price, all shape the effectiveness and sustainability of the risk transfer arrangement. A holistic evaluation across these dimensions ensures that risk is not only transferred but transferred well.

That said, selling your risk to an insurance company or third-party carrier has never been more challenging. Carrier capacity for risk is at an all-time low, while risk selectivity is at an all-time high, meaning that only the most carefully managed risks are considered attractive. To stand out, your business must present itself as the best of the best, demonstrating strong risk mitigation, loss control, and a willingness to accept higher deductibles or retentions. Just as important is how you communicate these efforts to the carrier, making it clear that your account is being actively managed to perform better than expected losses. Even with all of this in place, you must still be prepared for the realities of today's market, unjust denials, sudden nonrenewal, rate increases, and the turmoil that follows. In this environment, positioning your risk effectively is not just a matter of cost control, but of ensuring continued access to coverage itself.

Risk transfer does not always take the form of traditional insurance; there are numerous other mechanisms available, each with its own complexities. Indemnity clauses and carefully crafted contract language can shift liability to another party, but their enforceability often hinges on jurisdictional nuances and negotiation strength. Families should be aware that while business attorneys may be well-positioned to handle frequent legal needs, they often lack expertise in the specifics of indemnity provisions, as this is a specialized area of law typically regulated by legal professionals who focus on insurance indemnity, litigation, defense, or risk management.

Third-party risk financing arrangements, such as risk pools or structured products, allow organizations to share or outsource exposures, though they may involve significant capital commitments or counterparty risk. Group and single parent captive insurance companies create opportunities to retain and finance risk within a controlled structure, offering flexibility and potential tax efficiencies, but they require meaningful capitalization, regulatory compliance, and strong governance. In addition, self-insurance programs with reinsurance offer an alternative approach, allowing companies to fund their losses up to a specified threshold while securing coverage for catastrophic events. Fronting programs, in which an organization partners with a licensed insurer to issue policies while retaining much of the risk, offer a means to access markets and meet regulatory requirements without entirely relying on third-party insurers. Catastrophe bonds, derivatives, and reinsurance further spread risk across broader financial networks, ensuring that no single entity bears the full impact of a disaster. Government-backed programs, like the National Flood Insurance Program (NFIP) or state windstorm pools, provide additional layers of protection where private markets may fall short. By strategically leveraging these financial tools to transfer risk effectively, businesses and individuals transform uncertainty into manageable costs, creating resilience in an unpredictable world. The key lies in selecting appropriate coverage levels and understanding policy terms to ensure that the transferred risk aligns with the family's unique needs and Risk Tolerance.

While these tools expand the spectrum of options beyond insurance for risk transfer, they demand careful design, management, and legal oversight to avoid unintended gaps or disputes at the moment of loss.

4. Assumption: Accepting Calculated Risks

When the cost to transfer or mitigate exceeds the cost to absorb.

Assumption involves consciously accepting a risk after carefully evaluating its potential impact and the family's capacity to absorb possible losses. This strategy is suitable for risks with a low likelihood and minor potential implications compared to a family's financial and emotional ability to handle a loss, especially when the cost of mitigation or transfer is higher than the possible loss itself. Like other risk management strategies, assuming risk requires awareness of both known and unknown risks. It's crucial to weigh the cost-benefit analysis of deciding to assume a risk against the family's Emotional versus Physical Risk Tolerance. Families may have the physical (financial) means to manage a risk, but if their emotional tolerance is misaligned, they may regret their choice when the risk materializes.

Risk Assumption is a core tenet of any risk management strategy, involving accepting the potential losses associated with a specific risk rather than Avoiding, Mitigating, or Transferring it.

For example, a small business might assume the risk of minor equipment malfunctions rather than paying for comprehensive insurance. However, risk assumption becomes unwise when dealing with high-impact or catastrophic events with potentially devastating financial or reputational consequences. A company wouldn't reasonably assume the risk of a major environmental disaster or a massive data breach; instead, they'd leverage mitigation strategies and insurance to transfer such substantial risk. The decision to assume risk hinges on a careful evaluation of probability, potential severity, and available resources.

The Interplay of all Four Tools of Risk Management

As noted above, these tools do not frequently operate independently. Often, the choice to adopt one tool requires a thorough analysis of how that would impact the other three.

For example, an established franchised farm equipment distributor pays $2.5 million annually in insurance premiums to manage risk related to his business and inventory. He is considering increasing his deductible to reduce his premium expense, which would save him $40,000 per year, but increase his liability by $400,000 in the event of an adverse outcome. Financially, he can handle the high-frequency, low-severity events associated with this change, but he may not fully understand how his Emotional Risk Tolerance of saving money today influences his decision-making.

Often, his advisors fail to engage in candid discussions about the Emotional versus Physical Risk Tolerance as well as the true catastrophic exposures that could devastate his company and net worth. While he may achieve short-term insignificant savings by raising his deductible, the onset of high-frequency claims could lead to substantial out-of-pocket costs, ultimately leaving him dissatisfied with more out-of-pocket cost.

Another strategy, to enhance the efficiency of his risk transfer and adequately address 'enterprise' risk, would be for him to consider assuming all the risk associated with his equipment, inventory, and property or adopting a catastrophic loss policy potentially saving $1,000,000 in annual premium costs, at the same time repositioning coverage for Supply Chain Interruption, Loss of Franchise Agreement, and/or Regulatory Change; exposures which truly could be catastrophic. He has the financial capacity to replace his inventory, but he does not have the financial capacity to lose his franchise agreement or deal with the devastation of not securing inventory or parts due to a material supply chain issue. In this case, his risk focus is inverted, focusing on the low-probability, low-severity issues, opposed to the low-probability, high-severity ones. Adopting the alternative strategy would protect against potentially devastating impacts on his business and family's net worth. Failing to address upstream risks, such as supply chain interruptions properly, leaves the family with coverage for claims they can absorb but leaves them fully exposed to those that they potentially cannot.

This shift in the owner's perception regarding emotional versus Physical Risk Tolerance requires significant insight into his actual exposures. Without open dialogue with a qualified Risk Manager, he may unknowingly adopt a strategy that aligns more with his emotional concerns rather than his financial reality. A thorough analysis may have revealed that he is assuming more risk than he realizes, potentially exposing his net worth to catastrophic loss from unidentified enterprise risks.

Often this is a reality for people who have achieved significant success. During the years building the business, much of their risk is likely centered around commercial risks. Still, as the family's overall enterprise grows, the impact of loss at more material levels can be exponentially higher. Failure to assess and adjust risk management strategies related to all risks can lead to a significant loss, potentially wiping out the family's net worth entirely, as seen in the example of the ice cream manufacturer previously discussed.

By implementing a strategic and thoughtful approach to the four tools of risk management using the Total Family Balance Sheet framework, families and individuals can develop a strategy to offset the most detrimental impacts of Financial Gravity. Families must understand that often they have material exposures they aren't even aware of. The unknown assumption of risk is the single most significant force of potential Financial Gravity on a family's net worth.

Checklist & Key Questions

- Are we Informed about all of our potential exposures?
- Where are we relying on Emotional Risk Tolerance instead of real financial capacity?
- Which of our risks are we unknowingly assuming?
- Do we understand which risks we should be avoiding?

- Have we evaluated which risks we can more effectively assume or mitigate to reduce potential costs of risk transfer?
- Does the insurance company we selected have the financial capacity to meet our needs and those of their other policyholders in the event of a catastrophic event?
- Are our indemnity clauses optimized in our favor in all contracts?
- Are we efficiently transferring risk correlated to our cost-benefit analysis of a specific project or risk?

Conclusion
Utilizing the Four Tools of Risk Management within the Total Family Balance Sheet Framework

The assumption of unknown risk represents the most formidable force of Financial Gravity that individuals and families face in their financial journeys. As demonstrated through our exploration of risk management strategies, particularly in the context of high-stakes environments like that of the farm equipment distributor, it becomes evident that the actual danger lies not only in the risks we recognize but also in those lurking beneath the surface, risks that can escalate to catastrophic proportions if left unaddressed. As families grow and their enterprises expand, the potential impacts of loss become exponentially greater, threatening to erase years of hard-earned wealth. Without diligent assessment and open, candid, vulnerable conversations with knowledgeable advisors, families may unwittingly expose themselves to significant financial vulnerabilities. Therefore, it is imperative to cultivate a holistic understanding of both Emotional and Physical Risk Tolerance, ensuring a comprehensive approach to risk management that safeguards against the unseen forces that could jeopardize their family's financial legacy. By staying proactive and adaptable in their strategies, families can better navigate the complexities of risk and protect their future against the unanticipated challenges that may arise.

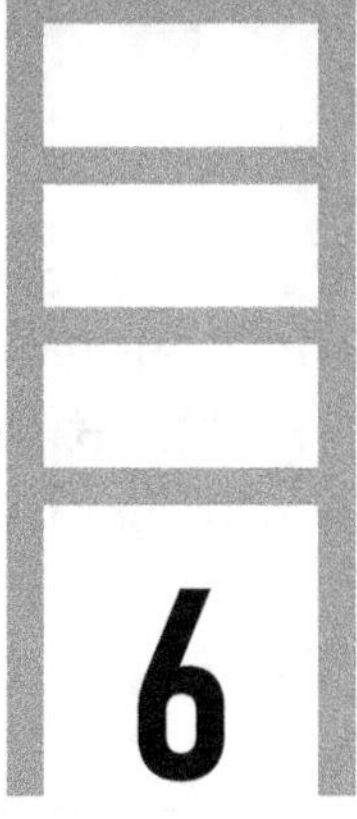

BALANCING RISK EXPOSURES
Low Severity vs. High Severity Events

In the dynamic landscape of personal finance and wealth management, understanding risk exposure is crucial for families striving to preserve their net worth and achieve long-term financial security. Utilizing the Total Family Balance Sheet framework, we can evaluate risk exposures by examining potential losses through the lens of frequency and severity (i.e. low-severity/high-frequency events, low-severity/low-frequency events, high-severity/low-frequency events, and high-severity/high-frequency events).

Families must be aware that from an actuarial science perspective (probability of a given loss occurring), the number of losses is referred to by risk industry professionals as 'frequency,' whereas the impact (financial, or otherwise) of a loss is identified as 'severity'.

When evaluating risk exposures, frequency and severity must always be considered in tandem, as their interaction ultimately determines both the financial impact of a loss and the appropriate strategy for managing it. A loss that occurs frequently but with low severity ('annoying') may be predictable and manageable through cash flow, while a loss that occurs rarely but carries high severity could threaten a family's entire financial foundation ('catastrophic') if not properly transferred or mitigated.

Understanding where a given risk falls on this spectrum helps families make Informed decisions about which risks are being retained, which to reduce, and which to transfer to third parties, ensuring their overall risk management approach aligns with both their Physical and Emotional tolerance for loss.

Figure 6.1 Annoying vs. Catastrophic: Reality of the interplay of frequency and severity of a loss.

The Actuarial Anomaly: Frequency and Severity

An intriguing aspect of risk management is understanding how the frequency of events can influence the likelihood of severity, an **Actuarial Anomaly** that professionals should be aware of. Intuitively, one might think that rare events pose less risk; however, the frequency of low-severity events can create a separate risk dynamic that can drive the likelihood of a catastrophic event. This is known to industry professionals as 'frequency drives severity'.

When families experience numerous low-severity events, they often become desensitized to the risks associated with them. This desensitization can lead to complacency, where families may neglect to address their risk management strategies thoughtfully. This misguided approach increases the likelihood that, when a high-severity event finally occurs, the family may be ill-prepared both financially and emotionally. The accumulation of minor but frequent disruptions can dilute the perceived Financial Gravity of risk, leading to a dangerous assumption that higher-severity events will have a less pronounced impact than they might truly entail.

To further complicate the analysis, families should consider concepts of a hazard in risk management. A hazard is any condition, behavior, or situation that increases the likelihood (frequency) or potential impact (severity) of a loss. It does not cause the loss itself: that role belongs to the peril (such as fire, theft, or illness), but rather a hazard makes the occurrence or outcome of that peril more probable or damaging. Hazards are generally categorized into four main types: physical hazards (tangible conditions like faulty wiring or icy roads), moral hazards (intentional risky behavior due to insulation from consequences), morale hazards (carelessness or indifference because of perceived protection), and legal hazards (changes in laws or legal environments that heighten liability exposure).

While applying the four tools of risk management is critical to managing risk related to physical and legal hazards, it is important to understand that moral and morale hazards are the two behavioral dimensions that can directly influence both the frequency and severity of loss. Moral hazard arises when an individual or entity intentionally behaves differently because they are insulated from the financial consequences of their actions, such as being less cautious because insurance coverage exists, potentially increasing both the frequency and severity of losses. Morale hazard, on the other hand, stems from carelessness or complacency rather than intent; it reflects a diminished sense of responsibility or vigilance simply because protection is perceived to exist. In the context of family wealth, these hazards are particularly relevant. When families possess significant financial resources, there can be a temptation or unconscious tendency to absorb losses directly rather than proactively manage or prevent them. While wealth can indeed cushion the impact of many losses, it should not replace disciplined risk management. Insurance should still be considered for high-severity events where even substantial family capital could be strained, ensuring that wealth serves as a tool for opportunity and legacy without fully exposing the family to potential impacts of Financial Gravity, not merely a backstop for preventable risks. Understanding and managing hazards and their impact on frequency and severity of loss is essential for effective risk mitigation, as they represent the underlying factors that magnify both the frequency and severity of potential losses.

Annoying Loss Events

High-frequency/low-severity events are occurrences that, while relatively minor individually, can accumulate to have a significant financial impact over time, and can be indicative of a more substantial loss to come. These events are characterized by their high probability of occurrence and lower potential impact per event. Simple examples include:

- Minor vehicle accidents
- Frequent home maintenance issues (e.g., plumbing leaks, roof repairs)
- Small health-related expenses (e.g., doctor visits, prescriptions)

Similarly, low-frequency/low-severity events are infrequent occurrences that create minor inconvenience or modest financial impact when they happen. Examples include a one-time appliance breakdown, a small tax penalty due to an oversight, or a single minor home repair such as a broken window.

From a risk management perspective, families frequently encounter these events. While the financial burden per occurrence may be manageable, the cumulative cost over time (for high-frequency events) or the occasional unexpected minor cost (for low-frequency events) can strain budgets and impact overall economic stability. Families must assess their ability to absorb these costs within their total financial balance, ensuring there are adequate funds and reserves set aside for ongoing or occasional expenses.

Catastrophic Loss Events

In contrast, low-frequency/high-severity events present a different type of risk exposure. These events are rare but carry catastrophic financial consequences when they do occur. Simple examples of low-frequency/high-severity events include:

- Major health crises (e.g., surgeries, chronic illness)
- Significant natural disasters (e.g., floods, fires)
- Economic downturns impacting employment or investments

In addition, high-frequency/high-severity events though rare, can combine to create extreme financial exposure. Examples might include repeated regulatory violations for a business resulting in escalating fines, ongoing litigation with multiple claims, or recurring catastrophic equipment failures in a high-risk industry. These events can quickly deplete resources and overwhelm risk management strategies if not properly mitigated or insured.

Families often underestimate or overlook the financial impact of both the frequency and severity of potential losses. For a risk management strategy to be effective, to provide the desired protection, and be truly satisfying, it must account for not only these loss characteristics but also the family's financial capacity and Emotional Risk Tolerance. What one family perceives as a minor annoyance, another may see as a catastrophic event. For example, a $5,000 fender-bender could be devastating for an independent financially strapped college student juggling daily expenses, while a multi-generational wealthy family might view the same cost as a mere inconvenience. Understanding these differences in perspective is critical for designing a risk management plan that aligns with both financial reality and emotional comfort.

Using the Total Family Balance Sheet framework, families can visualize the effects of both types of loss. The consistent costs associated with low severity events must be accounted for, ensuring that budgets allow for minor repairs and regular expenses. On the other hand, a robust contingency planning strategy, combined with the effective use of the **Four Tools of Risk Management**, can more comprehensively ensure the long-term success of a family. Advisors can help families determine whether each risk is being evaluated with Informed awareness or if critical blind spots exist.

Action Checklist

- Confirm adequate cash-reserves to cover the average of last three years high frequency/low severity costs in addition to your typical lifestyle reserve requirements.
- Stress-test your risk management strategies for potential outcomes of your top low frequency/high severity events; ensuring the strategy adequately meets those potential needs to offset the potential catastrophic hits from Financial Gravity.
- Align entity and trust structures with exposed assets and the most severe event with umbrella/excess catastrophe limits in the worst-case model.

Conclusion
Considering Frequency and Severity within the Total Family Balance Sheet Framework

A thorough understanding of risk exposure through the Total Family Balance Sheet framework enables families to navigate the complex interplay between low-frequency/low-severity, high-frequency/low-severity, low-frequency/high-severity and high-frequency/high-severity events. Through recognizing complexities such as the Actuarial Anomaly that frequency can influence severity, families can adopt more Informed risk management strategies. This holistic perspective will not only help protect their financial legacy but also help ensure stability in the face of uncertainty, transforming their approach to risk from one of reaction to one of preparedness.

In Part II of this book, we will unpack each Asset Silo, identify common exposures related to those assets, and provide techniques for practical guidance on how to manage risk properly.

PART II

EXPOSURES OF THE SIX ASSET SILOS OF THE TOTAL FAMILY BALANCE SHEET FRAMEWORK

Having explored the core elements of managing risk in Part I of this book, the following chapters will begin applying the whole framework to specific Asset Silos. Here, the entire process is brought to life by identifying commonly seen risks in a particular Asset Silo. Applying a family's Risk Tolerance, knowledge of a risk (i.e., Informed, Uninformed, Ill-Informed), establishing a risk's potential loss frequency and severity, and ultimately how you want to help protect your family by applying the four tools of risk management (Avoid, Transfer, Mitigate, or Assume).

The assets most highly successful families have fall into six key silos: investment portfolio, real estate, family operating business, private equity, personal assets, and family human capital. Contingent on the family situation, they may not have assets in all silos, but virtually everyone will have personal assets, and family human capital. Frequently, successful families will manage their exposure in one Asset Silo well, while neglecting others. A key objective of this framework is to provide the practical ability to comprehensively evaluate risk while promoting coordination and transparency across all silos.

True resilience stems from understanding how these Asset Silos interact and drive one another. Families should be using this framework to regularly examine how to manage their risk, influence their protection strategy, and make aligned informed decisions, ultimately helping to avoid Financial Gravity and preserve wealth across generations. This is where thoughtful planning, advisor coordination, and ongoing governance becomes real-world protection.

Figure Part II.1: *Deep dive into the exposures of the six Asset Silos of the Total Family Balance Sheet that most successful families and individuals hold.*

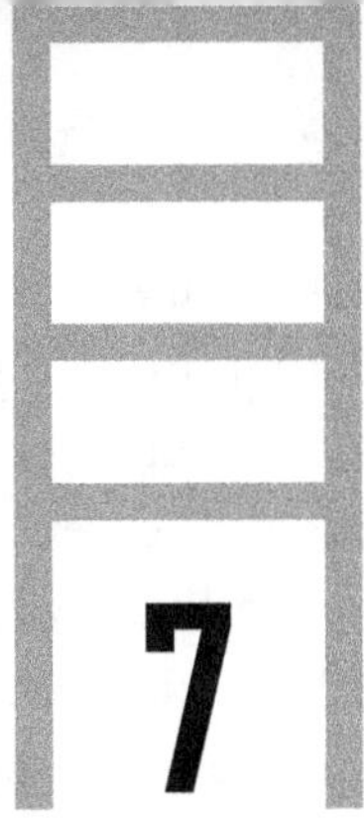

INVESTMENT PORTFOLIO
Analyzing Risks in Investment Portfolios

The investment portfolio represents a cornerstone of many high-net-worth families' financial holdings. While the management of this portfolio is typically handled by the family's chosen financial advisor, its integration within the Total Family Balance Sheet risk management framework serves a crucial, distinct purpose: to provide a comprehensive overview of the risks associated with the portfolio, ensuring those risks are properly considered within the context of the family's overall financial picture. All too often, the qualified investment advisor is working in their silo without understanding and communication of how the construction of an investment portfolio may impact, or be impacted, by the other Asset Silos. This chapter details how investment portfolio risk management analysis fits into the Total Family Balance Sheet Framework methodology.

It is essential to emphasize that this book, its contents, and the Total Family Balance Sheet framework are not intended to provide investment, legal, or tax advice of any kind. The Total Family Balance Sheet Framework doesn't aim to replace the expertise of a qualified financial advisor in portfolio construction or asset management. Instead, it leverages the advisor's expertise to enhance risk awareness, ensuring that the investment portfolio's inherent risks are accurately assessed and integrated into the family's overall risk profile while considering the risks that may be present in other Asset Silos.

As identified and shown in the image (7.1), we have curated a list of the most frequent associated risks families may want to consider related to investment portfolios. In the context of the family's investment portfolio, there can be many factors that determine what exposures are present, with every family's exposure likely varying greatly. With that said, Macroeconomic Risk, Asset Allocation and Asset Correlation, and Risk Diversification are the most commonly seen pitfalls of an uncoordinated risk management strategy.

Associated Risks	Informed	Uninformed	Avoid	Mitigate	Transfer	Assume
Audit	☐	☐	☐	☐	☐	☐
Basis	☐	☐	☐	☐	☐	☐
Concentration	☐	☐	☐	☐	☐	☐
Contract Dispute	☐	☐	☐	☐	☐	☐
Crisis	☐	☐	☐	☐	☐	☐
Cyber	☐	☐	☐	☐	☐	☐
Diversification	☐	☐	☐	☐	☐	☐
Fiduciary	☐	☐	☐	☐	☐	☐
Fraud	☐	☐	☐	☐	☐	☐
Governance	☐	☐	☐	☐	☐	☐
Inflation	☐	☐	☐	☐	☐	☐
Liquidity	☐	☐	☐	☐	☐	☐
Longevity	☐	☐	☐	☐	☐	☐
Market Risk	☐	☐	☐	☐	☐	☐
N&F Lawsuit	☐	☐	☐	☐	☐	☐
Political	☐	☐	☐	☐	☐	☐
Regulatory	☐	☐	☐	☐	☐	☐
Reinvestment	☐	☐	☐	☐	☐	☐
Suitability	☐	☐	☐	☐	☐	☐
Inventory / Supply chain	☐	☐	☐	☐	☐	☐
Terrorism	☐	☐	☐	☐	☐	☐
Time	☐	☐	☐	☐	☐	☐
Transfer	☐	☐	☐	☐	☐	☐
Volatility	☐	☐	☐	☐	☐	☐
Typical Across Institutions	☐	☐	☐	☐	☐	☐
Ad-Hoc	☐	☐	☐	☐	☐	☐
Reporting and Risks	☐	☐	☐	☐	☐	☐

Figure 7.1 Investment Portfolio Risk Matrix: *Mapping the Four Tools Across a Portfolio. This illustration maps specific investment exposures to the four tools of risk management (Avoidance, Mitigation, Transference or Assuption) and overlays Informed versus Uninformed awareness, helping families visualize which risks require strategic reclassification.*

Macroeconomic Risk: A comprehensive risk management strategy would include a detailed assessment of the various risks associated with the portfolio, including market risk, interest rate risk, credit risk, and liquidity risk. This includes evaluating the potential impact of various macroeconomic factors and global events.

Asset Allocation and Correlation: The Total Family Balance Sheet Framework considers asset allocation within the context of asset correlations across all family holdings, not just investments.

*Consider a market-wide small-cap downturn that can disproportionately impact a family with significant exposure in both their investment portfolios, small-cap positions, and their small-cap family operating business simultaneously. Unknowingly, the financial advisor has the family over-exposed in their managed brokerage assets to small-cap positions, when they have more than adequate exposure in that sector through the family operating business. This cascading effect, often overlooked in an uncoordinated, siloed approach to risk management, underscores the importance of **Holistic Wealth and Risk Management**.*

Risk Diversification: While many financial advisors emphasize investment portfolio diversification, the Total Family Balance Sheet Framework seeks to expand the purview of this concept to encompass risk diversification across all assets, liabilities, and off-balance-sheet exposures of an individual, family, or business.

A diversified investment portfolio may still leave a family vulnerable to risks such as legal exposure, environmental disasters, or reputational damage. Therefore, a holistic approach requires considering risk management across all Asset Silos and the multiple vectors of risk, including (but not limited to) geopolitical factors, market sectors, and asset classes, to create a financial picture more capable of withstanding the forces of Financial Gravity.

Inter-Silo Impact

It is easy in hindsight to write this example; the intention is to focus on how utilizing a framework like the Total Family Balance Sheet provides a much-needed checklist and guidance for ongoing risk management related to an Investment Portfolio.

Case in point, in the Spring of 2020, the World came to a screeching halt due to lockdowns and social distancing measures resulting from the impact of COVID-19. Take an advisor who has a significant position in a large-cap stock of a Detroit auto manufacturer that has historically performed very well, even in substantial market corrections (like the Great Recession, when they accepted no bailout money).

Contrary to what was initially projected at the beginning of the pandemic, the economic stimulus, increased savings, and the rise of auto transportation as the predominant form of travel led to a general boom in car sales.

This manufacturer initially enjoyed the run-up but quickly found itself in a supply chain crisis, unable to meet demand due to a shortage of essential microchips, sourced predominantly from East Asia, which were necessary to operate the newly manufactured vehicles. The manufacturer had tens of thousands of finished trucks, parked and ready to be sold, but they were handcuffed as they needed to install the crucial chip(s) to make them function. It's estimated that this supply chain risk was partially responsible for significant stock volatility, which led to a point where the stock plummeted by more than 45% and quarterly dividends were reduced to zero.

While there are no guarantees, the importance of a structured framework related to all aspects of risk management is critical, not just in initial decision-making, but also in ongoing re-evaluation. Had an advisor developed and used a coordinated framework like the Total Family Balance Sheet in their stock position selection they would have known to prioritize discussion related to risk of the position. This just may have led that the supply chain was not at risk before the COVID-19 crisis. In contrast, during the crisis, it may have been deemed unacceptable and have chosen to avoid the risk and change their position in the stock. As noted, hindsight is always 20/20; many investment managers are not communicating risk in a way that is consistent, coordinated, or easily understood by the family. Too often, the focus remains on performance, narratives, and market commentary, while the underlying exposures that truly matter are left unaddressed until a disruption forces the conversation. A disciplined framework creates a repeatable process to surface these risks early, stress test assumptions as conditions change, and ensure decisions are aligned with the family's broader objectives and risk tolerance. Ultimately, it is not about predicting the next crisis, but about building the governance and visibility needed to respond intelligently when the world inevitably shifts.

Checklist & Key Questions

By utilizing *The Total Family Balance Sheet by Higginbotham*™ checklist provided at the beginning of this chapter, a prudent Risk Manager can more comprehensively assess the risks associated with investment portfolios within a family's holdings and how to develop a strategy for addressing these potentialities.

- Are any investment exposures duplicating or amplifying risks that already exist in other Asset Silos across the Total Family Balance Sheet?
- Have we analyzed how current macroeconomic factors, such as interest rates, global events, and liquidity trends, could materially impact the portfolio?
- Does our asset allocation appropriately reflect the family's overall Risk Tolerance when viewed in coordination with operating businesses, real estate, and other holdings?
- Have we evaluated whether correlations between investments and non-investment assets create unintended concentration risks during periods of market stress?
- Is our portfolio's liquidity sufficient to meet short-term needs or obligations without requiring asset sales during unfavorable market conditions?

- Do we review financial advisor recommendations within the Total Family Balance Sheet framework to ensure they align with broader family objectives and risk posture?

Conclusion
Integrating Investment Portfolios into the Total Family Balance Sheet Framework

The key takeaway is that the analysis of the investment portfolio within the Total Family Balance Sheet framework isn't about recommending specific investments or managing the portfolio itself. Instead, it's about ensuring the family is fully aware of the risks associated with their investments and how those risks interact with other areas of their financial life. This holistic approach empowers families to make more Informed, strategic decisions, aligning their investment strategies with their overall Risk Tolerance and building a more resilient financial foundation. This integrated approach is crucial for navigating the complexities of modern wealth preservation and ensuring a secure future.

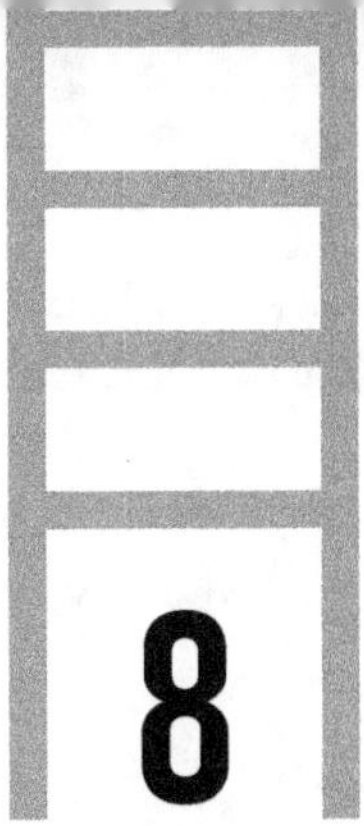

8

ANALYZING REAL ESTATE HOLDINGS

Bricks and Mortar, Risks and Rewards

Real estate often forms a significant component of successful families' assets, offering both substantial potential returns and considerable risk exposure. This chapter examines the intricacies of managing real estate holdings within the Total Family Balance Sheet framework, with a focus on identifying and mitigating potential liabilities.

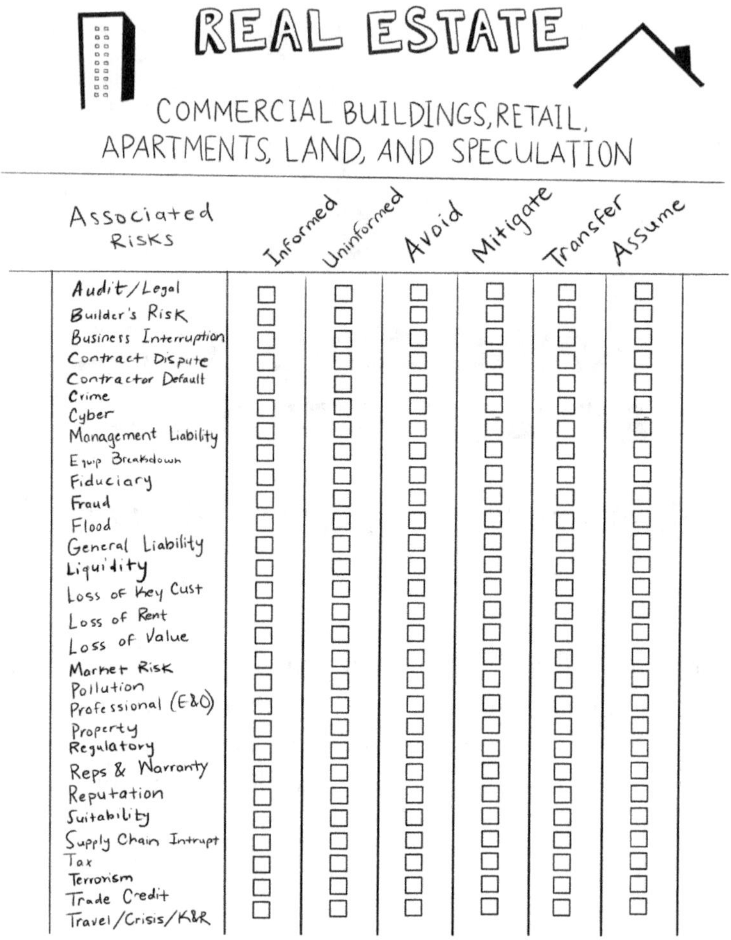

Associated Risks	Informed	Uninformed	Avoid	Mitigate	Transfer	Assume
Audit/Legal	☐	☐	☐	☐	☐	☐
Builder's Risk	☐	☐	☐	☐	☐	☐
Business Interruption	☐	☐	☐	☐	☐	☐
Contract Dispute	☐	☐	☐	☐	☐	☐
Contractor Default	☐	☐	☐	☐	☐	☐
Crime	☐	☐	☐	☐	☐	☐
Cyber	☐	☐	☐	☐	☐	☐
Management Liability	☐	☐	☐	☐	☐	☐
Equip Breakdown	☐	☐	☐	☐	☐	☐
Fiduciary	☐	☐	☐	☐	☐	☐
Fraud	☐	☐	☐	☐	☐	☐
Flood	☐	☐	☐	☐	☐	☐
General Liability	☐	☐	☐	☐	☐	☐
Liquidity	☐	☐	☐	☐	☐	☐
Loss of Key Cust	☐	☐	☐	☐	☐	☐
Loss of Rent	☐	☐	☐	☐	☐	☐
Loss of Value	☐	☐	☐	☐	☐	☐
Market Risk	☐	☐	☐	☐	☐	☐
Pollution	☐	☐	☐	☐	☐	☐
Professional (E&O)	☐	☐	☐	☐	☐	☐
Property	☐	☐	☐	☐	☐	☐
Regulatory	☐	☐	☐	☐	☐	☐
Reps & Warranty	☐	☐	☐	☐	☐	☐
Reputation	☐	☐	☐	☐	☐	☐
Suitability	☐	☐	☐	☐	☐	☐
Supply Chain Intrupt	☐	☐	☐	☐	☐	☐
Tax	☐	☐	☐	☐	☐	☐
Terrorism	☐	☐	☐	☐	☐	☐
Trade Credit	☐	☐	☐	☐	☐	☐
Travel/Crisis/K&R	☐	☐	☐	☐	☐	☐

Figure 8.1 Real Estate Risk Map: Applying the four tools across a property demonstrates how a prudent Risk Manager evaluates a property's exposures using the Total Family Balance Sheet lens: Informed vs. Uninformed awareness, matched with the four tools of risk management (Avoidance, Mitigation, Transference, or Assumption).

Beyond Market Value: A Multifaceted Risk Assessment

The traditional valuation of real estate often overlooks the multifaceted nature of the risks associated with it. While market fluctuations undoubtedly play a significant role, a comprehensive risk assessment must extend far beyond simple price movements to encompass a broader range of potential liabilities, including, but not limited to, those expounded below:

Market Fluctuations: Real estate values are subject to cyclical market trends and influenced by macroeconomic factors, including interest rates, inflation, population changes, and economic growth. A downturn in the market can significantly reduce property values, affect the family's overall net worth, and potentially create liquidity challenges.

Real Estate Market + Leverage = Solvency Risk

Leverage risk is a critical subcomponent of market risk in real estate, amplifying the effects of market fluctuations on an investor's equity and/or cash flow. When property values decline and/or vacancies occur, highly leveraged investors face a disproportionate reduction in their equity position and potentially their returns. The fixed nature of debt obligations, property tax liabilities, and maintenance remains unavoidable and potentially increasing at a time when cash flow from the asset may be declining.

Among the many potential risks associated with leverage, in a general market downturn, investors can find themselves in situations where the loan balance exceeds the property's market value, leaving the investor "underwater." Compounding this is the impact of interest rate risk, where rising interest rates increase borrowing costs, particularly for variable-rate loans, further squeezing cash flow and profitability. Declining rental income during economic downturns can exacerbate these challenges, making it harder to service debt and meet other financial obligations. The interplay between leverage, market risk, and interest rate risk underscores the importance of prudent borrowing strategies, as even minor market or rate shifts can have a significant impact on highly leveraged investments, ultimately affecting liquidity and potential solvency.

Owning real estate exposes families to significant liability risks. This includes personal injury claims arising from accidents on the property, legal disputes with tenants or neighbors, Reputational Risk, and environmental liabilities resulting from property contamination.

Regulatory risk in real estate refers to the uncertainty and potential financial impact caused by changes in laws, regulations, or government policies that affect property ownership, development, and operations. This risk can arise from zoning law adjustments, building code revisions, environmental regulations, or changes in property tax rates.

Vacancy risk is one of the most persistent and underestimated exposures within real estate holdings, encompassing both financial and physical dimensions of loss. When a property remains unoccupied, whether due to market conditions, tenant turnover, or management issues, the result can be a significant loss of income and asset value. Even brief vacancies can strain cash flow as fixed expenses such as taxes, insurance, and maintenance continue without offsetting revenue, while extended vacancies may depress valuations, trigger loan covenant breaches, and reduce overall liquidity across the family's Total Family Balance Sheet. Beyond financial loss, vacant properties face heightened exposure to vandalism, theft, fire, and water damage, risks that often go unnoticed without regular occupancy and oversight. These exposures can erode property value and insurability, as carriers may restrict coverage or raise deductibles once a property is deemed vacant. Proactive leasing strategies, geographic diversification, robust security, regular inspections, and adequate reserves are all essential to managing vacancy risk effectively. Ultimately, safeguarding against both the economic and physical threats of vacancy is vital to preserving the long-term stability and value of real estate portfolios.

Coastal and Wildfire Insurance Spiral

A growing concern in many states like Florida, Louisiana, Colorado, Texas, and California is the impact of insurance regulations, and rising premiums driven by natural disasters, such as hurricanes, wildfires, and floods. These increases can significantly inflate property ownership costs, reduce net operating income, and deter potential buyers or tenants. Stricter insurance requirements and reduced coverage availability exacerbate the issue, leaving property owners vulnerable to greater financial losses. For investors and developers, such shifts can complicate project feasibility and long-term profitability. Navigating this landscape requires proactive risk management, including staying informed about regional policy changes and incorporating higher insurance costs into financial planning.

Business Interruption & Loss of Income Risk

Beyond the direct costs of repairing physical damage, the interruption of operations or income following a major event can have lasting and far-reaching consequences. When a property or business is disrupted by fire, flood, storm, or another catastrophe, the physical structures may be restorable, but the resulting disruption to revenue and productivity often takes much longer to recover. Effective risk management requires planning not only for immediate physical restoration, but also for operational continuity and financial resilience.

When a natural disaster or regional crisis fundamentally alters a community's size or economic activity (through population shifts, reduced commerce, or infrastructure loss), the consequences can extend well beyond the recovery period. Local demand for housing, retail, or services may decline permanently, leaving rebuilt enterprises struggling to regain prior performance levels. This underscores the importance of evaluating disruption exposure through the combined lenses of market resilience, community recovery, and sustainable income stability. Integrating these considerations into a comprehensive risk management framework ensures families and enterprises can withstand both the immediate shock and the enduring economic effects of major disruptions.

Property Management & Tax Exposure Risk

Managing real property introduces a wide spectrum of operational, financial, and human-factor risks. Effective oversight requires careful selection and supervision of property managers, clear tenant management practices, enforceable lease structures, and reliable systems for maintenance and repairs. Breakdowns in any of these areas can lead to declining asset performance, manifesting as reduced cash flow, unexpected expenses, property deterioration, or even litigation. From a risk management perspective, families must recognize that poorly governed property operations can erode both the immediate income and long-term value of an asset, making proactive oversight and structured governance essential.

Real estate holdings also carry significant tax-related risks that can materially influence overall returns. Property taxes, capital gains exposure, depreciation schedules, and jurisdiction-specific rules all shape the economic outcome of an investment. Without proper planning, these obligations can create liquidity strains, diminish net proceeds, or unintentionally accelerate tax liabilities. Strong risk management requires understanding the full tax landscape surrounding each property and integrating it into the broader financial strategy, ensuring that the family optimizes after-tax outcomes while reducing the potential for avoidable surprises.

A Proactive, Comprehensive Approach to Real Estate Risk Management

The Total Family Balance Sheet framework emphasizes a proactive, comprehensive approach to mitigating real estate risks. This involves a combination of strategies tailored to the specific properties, professional coordination, and the family's overall Risk Tolerance, some of which are listed below:

- **Insurance:** Comprehensive insurance coverage is crucial for protecting against property damage, liability claims, loss of income, regulatory changes, and other unforeseen events.
- **Legal Counsel:** Engaging experienced legal counsel to review and ensure compliance with all relevant regulations and legal requirements is paramount. This includes reviewing leases, contracts, property ownership, and most importantly understanding terms related to mutual indemnification in all agreements.

- **Professional Management:** Investing in and properly utilizing experienced and reputable property managers to oversee day-to-day operations, tenant management, and maintenance can substantially mitigate the risks associated with owning rental properties.

- **Due Diligence:** A comprehensive due-diligence process is one of the most critical components of real estate risk management. Before acquiring any property, families must thoroughly evaluate the physical, legal, regulatory, and financial conditions that could influence long-term performance or introduce unforeseen liability. This includes professional property inspections, environmental assessments, zoning and land-use reviews, title examinations, lease audits for income-producing assets, and a clear understanding of outstanding permits or code-compliance obligations. Proper due diligence must also assess the property's vulnerability to physical damage loss, including exposure to natural hazards (e.g., flood zones, wildfire risk, seismic activity), aging infrastructure, prior maintenance deficiencies, and the availability and cost of risk-transfer solutions. Overlooking these issues can result in catastrophic repair costs the inability to rebuild or replace a structure due to regulatory changes, prolonged downtime, impaired income, or long-term devaluation.

Figure 8.2 Examining the risks associated with real estate holdings through a magnified risk management lens.

Many properties also rely on historical "grandfathered" rights (such as out-dated building codes, nonconforming uses, or prior entitlements) that may not transfer to a new owner or may be revoked upon renovation, change of use, or regulatory updates. Failure to account for these exposures can create substantial and unplanned capital requirements, delayed operations, and significant risk to projected financial outcomes.

A brief example: A family purchases a mixed-use building whose upper floors were legally used as short-term rentals under previously grandfathered zoning rules. After acquisition, the city updates its ordinances, eliminating the non-conforming use and requiring the new owner to comply with current lodging and fire-safety standards. At the same time, a detailed structural assessment, conducted only after closing, reveals outdated electrical systems that materially increase fire risk. The result is hundreds of thousands of dollars in mandatory upgrades, increased vulnerability to physical damage loss, and a meaningful reduction in projected rental income, outcomes that could have been anticipated and priced into the transaction through proper due diligence.

Successful individuals and families often participate in real estate through limited partnerships, gaining access to large or sophisticated projects while remaining insulated from the full depth of due diligence typically performed by the general partner. While this structure can provide convenience and diversification, it also means limited partners must rely heavily on the sponsor's expertise, transparency, and risk management, underscoring the importance of selecting partners with strong governance, aligned incentives, and a disciplined approach to evaluating risk. Families must look at the Off-balance-sheet-liabilities of a partnership through the lens of the idea that general partners, motivated to attract investment, may emphasize a project's strengths (projected returns, location advantages, or development potential) while downplaying or minimizing certain risks or exposures. This dynamic reinforces the need for independent assessment and disciplined risk evaluation, even when investing through trusted partners.

Robust pre-acquisition due diligence not only reduces the likelihood of costly surprises but also enables families to make Informed decisions within the Total Family Balance Sheet framework, ensuring that each property aligns with their broader risk posture and long-term objectives.

Asset Correlation Risk Exposure: Integrating real estate holdings into the family's overall plan ensures they align with broader Risk Tolerance, liquidity needs, and long-term objectives, not only within the real estate silo but across the entire Total Family Balance Sheet. This includes evaluating how real estate exposures correlate with other asset classes, as cross-silo risks can compound unexpectedly; for example, a family heavily invested in new multifamily developments may also hold substantial equity positions in building-materials companies, creating concentrated vulnerability to the same market cycles. By assessing these interdependencies, families can better understand how real estate contributes to overall economic resilience and adjust their strategy to mitigate correlated risks.

Off-Balance-Sheet Risk Informed Decision-Making Pays Off

Consider a real scenario involving a family known to the authors who purchased an investment property on Florida's West Coast, located on a canal with substantial mooring capacity, with the intent to buy and hold for long-term appreciation while using vacation rentals to offset carrying costs. Prior to acquisition, the family used the Total Family Balance Sheet by Higginbotham Real Estate exposure checklist to evaluate potential exposures. Through this process, they identified two material risks: (1) emerging regulatory pressure that could restrict short-term rentals, and (2) instability in the Florida insurance market, where multiple carriers were withdrawing due to dysfunction within the state's regulatory environment. Both risks carried the potential to meaningfully affect future revenue and expenses.

Figure 8.3 Regulatory Risk in Action: Florida's Insurance and Rental Shocks Case study visualization showing how unexpected changes in state-level insurance and rental regulation can transform a high-potential asset into a liability. Highlights the impact of compounded risk exposure.

Because the family conducted thorough pre-purchase due diligence, they entered the deal fully Informed and prepared. They chose to limit CapEx improvements, recognizing that the long-term appreciation of waterfront land, not home upgrades, was likely to be the dominant driver of value. This approach allowed them to reduce additional financial exposure while keeping optionality intact if regulatory or insurance conditions worsened.

Ultimately, both risks materialized. Regulators imposed a vacation-rental ban requiring minimum 31-day stays, and insurance premiums doubled over three years. With revenue reduced and operating costs escalating, the property no longer aligned with the family's investment thesis. Relying on their predetermined plan, they elected to sell. While the asset did not achieve its full envisioned income potential, the family still realized a meaningful capital gain.

Shortly after the sale, Hurricane Ian struck the region, severely dam-aging the property. Friends commented that the family was "lucky" to have sold when they did. In reality, their outcome was not luck but the product of disciplined risk management. By evaluating exposures in advance, understanding their Emotional and Financial Risk Tolerance, and acting decisively when conditions shifted, they created the conditions for a successful, and satisfying, investment result despite uncontrollable external events.

Checklist & Key Questions

By utilizing *The Total Family Balance Sheet by Higginbotham™ checklist* provided at the beginning of this chapter, a prudent Risk Manager can more comprehensively assess the risks associated with real estate in a family's holdings and develop a strategy for addressing these potentialities.

- Have we evaluated how this real estate holding correlates with other assets across the Total Family Balance Sheet, and whether it introduces concentrated or overlapping risks?
- Can our family comfortably withstand periods of reduced cash flow, rising interest rates, or prolonged vacancies without straining liquidity or other Asset Silos?
- Have we assessed the property's exposure to regulatory changes, zoning shifts, environmental requirements, or the loss of grandfathered rights that could materially affect its performance?
- Do we have strong governance and oversight in place to ensure that management, maintenance, tenant relations, and compliance are effectively handled?
- Have we thoroughly evaluated the property's physical condition, hazard exposures, and potential for costly structural or environmental issues?
- Have we modeled how various adverse scenarios could impact this property and our broader holdings, and do we have a clear, predetermined strategy for when to hold, improve, or exit?

Conclusion
Integrating Real Estate into the Total Family Balance Sheet Framework

The Total Family Balance Sheet Framework doesn't merely list exposures; it's a dynamic assessment of risks and liabilities and encourages coordination between professional advisors. By integrating a comprehensive analysis of real estate holdings, including potential market fluctuations and Off-balance-sheet-liabilities, the framework provides a holistic view of the family's overall exposure and how it builds, executes, and optimizes a risk management strategy. This enables a more informed and strategic approach to managing this crucial asset class, aligning strategy with the family's Risk Tolerance and ensuring the long-term preservation of their wealth. The framework empowers families to make informed decisions, maximizing the potential returns while proactively mitigating potential risks.

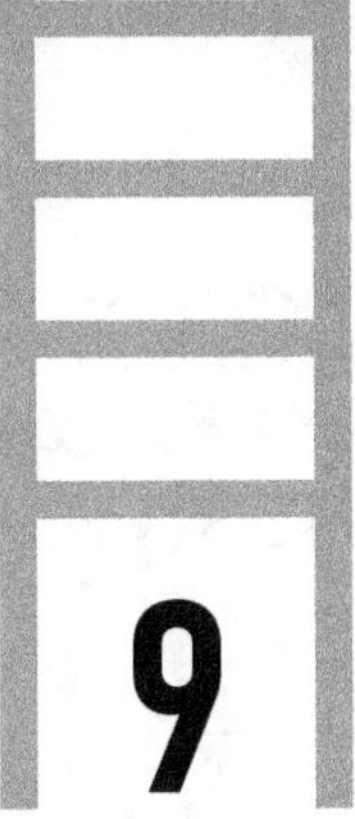

ASSESSING FAMILY OPERATING BUSINESSES

The Heart of the Matter

For many successful families, the family business forms the very core of their wealth and legacy. While often a significant source of pride and financial success, family businesses also present unique and substantial risks. This chapter examines how the Total Family Balance Sheet framework enables families to comprehensively assess these risks and opportunities, promoting long-term sustainability and ensuring a successful transition to future generations.

FAMILY Operating Business

FAMILY BUSINESS CONTROL

Associated Risks	Informed	Uninformed	Avoid	Mitigate	Transfer	Assume
Advertising	☐	☐	☐	☐	☐	☐
Aircraft	☐	☐	☐	☐	☐	☐
Audit/Legal	☐	☐	☐	☐	☐	☐
Auto	☐	☐	☐	☐	☐	☐
Bailees	☐	☐	☐	☐	☐	☐
Benefits & EP Liability	☐	☐	☐	☐	☐	☐
Brand	☐	☐	☐	☐	☐	☐
Business Interruption	☐	☐	☐	☐	☐	☐
Cargo	☐	☐	☐	☐	☐	☐
Contract Dispute	☐	☐	☐	☐	☐	☐
Contractual Liability	☐	☐	☐	☐	☐	☐
Crime	☐	☐	☐	☐	☐	☐
Cyber	☐	☐	☐	☐	☐	☐
Fiduciary	☐	☐	☐	☐	☐	☐
Flood	☐	☐	☐	☐	☐	☐
Foreign Liability	☐	☐	☐	☐	☐	☐
Fraud	☐	☐	☐	☐	☐	☐
General Liability	☐	☐	☐	☐	☐	☐
Intellectual Property	☐	☐	☐	☐	☐	☐
Inventory/Supply Chain	☐	☐	☐	☐	☐	☐
Loss of Bonding/Credit	☐	☐	☐	☐	☐	☐
Loss of Franchise	☐	☐	☐	☐	☐	☐
Loss of Key Cust	☐	☐	☐	☐	☐	☐
Loss of License	☐	☐	☐	☐	☐	☐
Management	☐	☐	☐	☐	☐	☐
Pollution	☐	☐	☐	☐	☐	☐
Products/Recall	☐	☐	☐	☐	☐	☐
Professional (E&O)	☐	☐	☐	☐	☐	☐
Property	☐	☐	☐	☐	☐	☐
Regulatory	☐	☐	☐	☐	☐	☐
Reputation	☐	☐	☐	☐	☐	☐
Succession	☐	☐	☐	☐	☐	☐
Terrorism	☐	☐	☐	☐	☐	☐
Trade Credit	☐	☐	☐	☐	☐	☐
Travel/Crisis/K&R	☐	☐	☐	☐	☐	☐
Warranty	☐	☐	☐	☐	☐	☐
Worker's Compensation	☐	☐	☐	☐	☐	☐

Figure 9.1: Family Operating Business - *Core Risk Considerations, outlines common exposures unique to family-owned enterprises, categorized across strategic, operational, financial, and relational risks, mapped to the four tools of risk management (Avoidance, Mitigation, Transference, or Assumption).*

Famous Family Business Failures

Throughout history, numerous prominent families have suffered devastating financial losses when the companies they owned or operated failed. The Vanderbilt family, once among the wealthiest in America due to their transportation empire is said to have been squandered their fortune over generations through lavish spending and poor reinvestment, leaving their legacy more symbolic than financial. The Lehman family, founders of the iconic investment bank Lehman Brothers, saw their name tarnished when the firm collapsed during the 2008 financial crisis, marking one of the most significant corporate failures in history. Similarly, the Astor family, once synonymous with New York City real estate, is said to have lost their empire through mismanagement and the pressures of maintaining extravagant lifestyles. In recent times, the Sears family witnessed the retail giant they built decline into bankruptcy, eroding both their wealth and legacy. Whether through mismanagement, a lack of diversification, or an inability to adapt to changing markets, these stories highlight the unique vulnerabilities of family-owned businesses and the lasting impact their failures can have on wealth, reputation, and future generations.

Beyond Profitability: A Multifaceted Risk Assessment

Traditional business valuations often focus solely on profitability and market value, overlooking the multifaceted risks inherent in family-owned enterprises, particularly since these businesses typically operate over a long-term horizon. The Total Family Balance Sheet Framework approach takes a more holistic view. There are numerous risk-related considerations in this silo, so we have highlighted a few that most family businesses are likely to encounter. A comprehensive analysis should be conducted in collaboration with the family business's Risk Manager and other advisors, considering the potential for Informed, Uninformed, or Ill-Informed decision-making, and utilizing the four tools for managing risk through Avoidance, Mitigation, Transference, or Assumption.

Strengthening the Family Enterprise Through Intentional Succession Planning

A key and often overlooked risk to a family enterprise lies in the absence of a well-defined succession plan. Without clarity around leadership and ownership transition, the family's entire net worth can be exposed to disruption, as the operating business is often a central, highly concentrated asset within the family's total balance sheet. Lacking intentional governance and communication, families can face internal conflict, liquidity strain, and misalignment in financial and Emotional Risk Tolerance. As outlined in the Preface, history will tell us of families once listed among the Forbes 400 who lost their financial empire, demonstrating how even great fortunes can fracture when critical factors like succession planning are neglected or delayed.

Proactive succession planning transforms this vulnerability into resilience. The Total Family Balance Sheet framework encourages families to design coordinated, cross-silo strategies that integrate financial, operational, and estate planning objectives. A comprehensive plan should anticipate leadership transitions, ownership changes, and the implications of retirement, death, or disability of key stakeholders. Beyond continuity, effective planning promotes harmony among family members, helps preserve enterprise value, and may further safeguard the legacy for future generations.

While this may seem a simple and obvious need for families, one that many people feel they have completed, far too often the succession plan is either inadequate, fragmented, and/or not formally documented. This planning deficiency can lead many family businesses lacking critical governance structures for a successful succession plan.

Equity Transition Planning in Family-Owned Enterprises

In the broader context of family succession planning, few areas carry greater long-term impact than equity transition planning. For most families, the operating business represents both a source of identity and a concentrated form of wealth, making the continuity of ownership and leadership essential. A well-designed transition framework should address several key areas, included but not limited to:

- **Valuation of Ownership Interests:** Establishing a clear, agreed-upon valuation method helps prevent disputes and ensures equitable treatment among family members and other key stakeholders.
- **Funding Mechanics:** Identifying how the ownership transition will be financed, through liquidity reserves, insurance funding, or other instruments, provides certainty and stability when a triggering event occurs.
- **Ownership Transfer Process:** Clearly outlining the procedures for ownership and management transfer minimizes disruption and supports operational continuity.
- **Tax Considerations:** Proper planning can reduce or defer tax liabilities, preserving both capital and family wealth across generations. All tax matters should always be addressed with the family's CPA, tax strategist, and a competent tax attorney.
- **Business Continuity:** Above all, the goal is to maintain the health and stability of the business through leadership transitions, ensuring that family legacy and enterprise value remain aligned.

Buy/Sell Planning Fundamentals

A Buy/Sell agreement, typically outlined in the business's operating agreement, is a legally binding contract that outlines the terms under which ownership interests will be transferred among the business owners (often family members) and key stakeholders. This is essential to prevent disputes and ensure a fair valuation during a succession event (death, disability, or retirement of an owner). There are several types of Buy/Sell agreements, each with different implications for tax and business operations:

- **Redemption:** The business buys out the departing owner's shares.
- **Cross-Purchase:** The remaining owners buy out the departing owner's shares.
- **Combination:** A hybrid approach using elements of both redemption and cross-purchase agreements.

Buy-Sell Funding Options

Frequently, families have a succession plan in mind, sometimes clearly documented, but the funding of that plan is not considered. This lack of a funding mechanism is a crucial consideration, as it can be the driving force behind challenges related to business operations and/or divisions within the family.

Typically, there are five funding mechanisms families will use to fund buy-outs: Sinking Fund (capital reserved to fund these events), Pay-As-You-Go (using the business's operating cash flow to fund), financing (using borrowed money to fund the need), taking on outside equity investment (i.e. family office capital, private equity), and finally, using the leverage of life insurance (either cash paid or premium financed to pay premium obligations).

Each of these options should be considered carefully, and may evolve over time.

As discussed in the Inverted Risk Focus framework, many families overlook the most certain and impactful risk, death. While transitions through retirement can often be managed with foresight and time, an unexpected death can instantly disrupt even the most carefully constructed succession plan. For this reason, funding business continuity through life insurance is often a prudent and strategic consideration. When properly structured, life insurance not only provides immediate liquidity in the event of premature death but can also serve as a stabilizing asset in planned transitions, supporting both business continuity and family harmony across generations.

Without properly structured life insurance strategies in the event of an untimely death, the company might need to take out a loan, sell assets, or bring on unplanned outside equity partners, potentially harming the family business' long-term financial health. The life insurance policy's death benefit may help provide the necessary capital to purchase the departing owner's shares, preventing the business from needing to secure financing or liquidate assets during a difficult time. The type of life insurance policy used (e.g., term, whole life) depends on the specific needs and economic circumstances of the business and its owners at the time of purchase.

Figure 9.2 Succession Planning: *A risk management strategy to help manage ownership changes through buy-sell structures (cross-purchase, redemption, or hybrid) that align with funding strategies such as insurance, cash reserves, equity, or debt.*

Key Person Planning

Key Person planning is a risk management strategy used by businesses, particularly family-owned ones, to mitigate the financial consequences of the death or disability of a key employee or family member who is crucial to the company's operations. It's designed to protect against the loss of revenue, expertise, and productivity that would result from such an event.

Key Person planning is a vital component that should be integrated into succession planning, enabling businesses to prepare financially for leadership changes. This approach provides resources for training new personnel and potentially facilitates a smooth transition of ownership.

Integrating the Family Business into the Total Family Balance Sheet Framework

The integration of family business assessments within the Total Family Balance Sheet framework provides several critical benefits:

- **Holistic Perspective:** It allows for a comprehensive understanding of the family business's contribution to the family's overall financial picture, highlighting both its potential and its vulnerabilities.
- **Proactive Risk Management and Advisor Coordination:** This approach encourages a proactive approach to identifying and mitigating risks associated with the business, thereby minimizing the potential for significant financial losses. Furthermore, given that the family business often represents a large proportion of a family's net worth, it is mission-critical that all advisors, across all silos, be intimately familiar with its happenings so they can adequately plan with consideration of this Asset Silo.
- **Strategic Planning:** It facilitates strategic planning for succession, operational improvements, and liability management, ensuring the long-term viability and success of the business.
- **Informed Decision-Making:** It empowers family members to make well informed decisions about the business's future, aligning their strategies with their overall financial goals and Risk Tolerance.

The Case for Planning

The failure of a nationally recognized hibachi restaurant's succession plan following the death of its founder highlights the risks associated with poor family governance and inadequate planning in family-owned businesses. The founder's lack of a clearly defined Buy/Sell agreement or succession strategy led to bitter disputes among his children over control of the company. These internal conflicts undermined the company's stability and created operational distractions at a critical time when the business needed cohesive leadership to navigate its competitive industry. Ultimately, the family's inability to resolve these issues forced the sale of the restaurant to private equity firms in 2012, marking the end of the family's control over the iconic restaurant chain. This example highlights the importance of developing comprehensive succession plans and enforceable Buy/Sell agreements that address ownership transitions, ensure leadership continuity, and establish effective dispute resolution mechanisms to safeguard a company's future.

Checklist & Key Questions

By utilizing *The Total Family Balance Sheet by Higginbotham*™ checklist provided at the beginning of this chapter allows for a more comprehensive approach to how a prudent Risk Manager would assess the risks associated with a family operating business within a family's holdings and how to develop a strategy for addressing these potentialities.

- Have we clearly defined and formally documented our leadership and ownership succession plan to avoid disruption during a transition?
- Do we have an agreed-upon valuation method and funding strategy to support an orderly and financially stable equity transition when a triggering event occurs?
- Have we identified, protected, and planned for the potential loss or disability of key people whose absence would materially affect operations or enterprise value?
- Are we proactively addressing strategic, operational, financial, and relational risks that could threaten business continuity or family harmony?
- Is the family business fully integrated into the Total Family Balance Sheet so that all advisors understand its concentration risk, liquidity needs, and cross-silo implications?
- Have we established governance structures, communication protocols, and dispute-resolution mechanisms to prevent family conflict from undermining the business?

Conclusion

For many successful families, the operating business is the core asset on the Total Family Balance Sheet. It is often the largest concentration of wealth, the greatest source of pride, and the single most important driver of legacy. That also makes it one of the most significant sources of risk.

By integrating the family business assessment into the Total Family Balance Sheet Framework, families gain a disciplined way to evaluate more than just profitability and valuation. They are able to identify strategic, operational, financial, and relational exposures that can quietly compound over time, especially when leadership transitions, liquidity demands, or family dynamics create pressure on the enterprise.

Most family business failures are not caused by one dramatic event. They are caused by incomplete planning, unclear governance, and a lack of coordination across advisors and asset silos. Succession plans without structure create disruption. Buy-sell agreements without funding create conflict. Key-person risk without protection creates instability at the worst possible moment.

The Total Family Balance Sheet Framework provides a practical, proactive approach to managing these realities. It creates visibility, improves decision-making, strengthens continuity, and helps families protect what they have built. When the family business is treated as an integrated component of the full balance sheet, rather than an isolated silo, families are far more likely to preserve enterprise value, maintain harmony, and successfully transition wealth and leadership to the next generation.

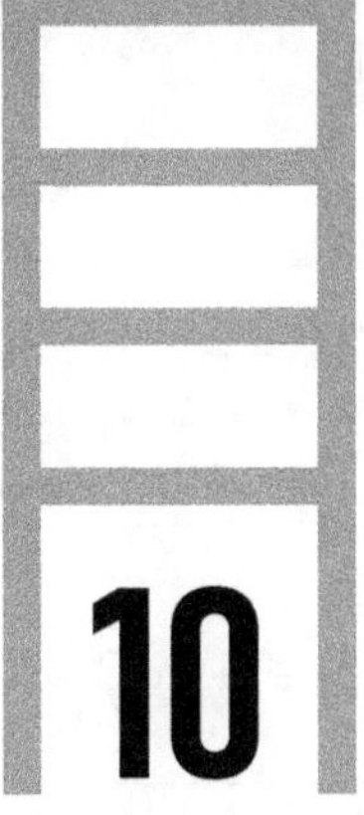

10

PRIVATE EQUITY INVESTMENTS
Managing Hidden Risks

Direct Private equity investments, while offering the potential for substantial returns, present unique complexities and significant risks. This chapter explores these complexities within the context of the Total Family Balance Sheet Framework, focusing on identifying, assessing, and managing risks from the perspectives of Informed, Ill-Informed, and Uninformed stakeholders, and through the strategic application of the four tools of risk management: Avoidance, Mitigation, Transfer, or Assumption.

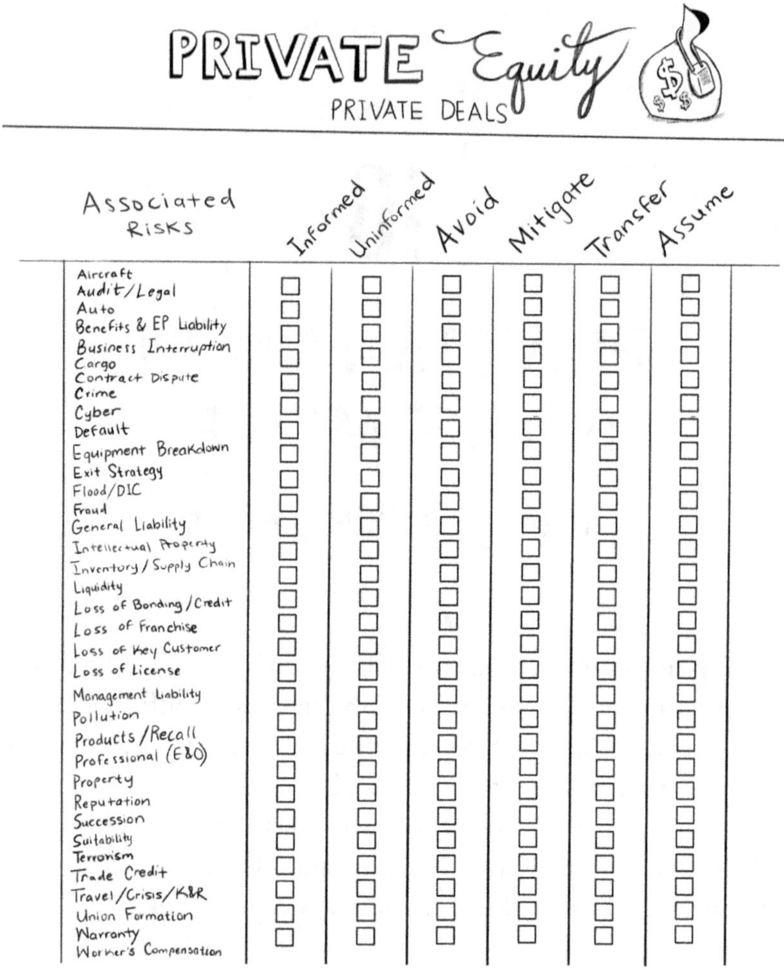

Figure 10.1 Private Equity Risk Framework: *A risk classification matrix showing how private equity risks can be assessed across Informed/ Uninformed axes and matched with the four tools of risk strategy.*

The Allure and the Risks of Private Equity

Private equity investments often attract high net worth individuals and families due to their potential for high returns.

Comparison: Family Operating Own PE Fund vs. Investing in One

When deciding between running an individual operating private equity fund (direct investment) or investing in an established private equity fund (indirect investment), families must weigh the trade-offs in risk management, due diligence, and operational involvement. Operating a private equity fund provides the family with complete control over investments, enabling tailored strategies that align with their unique objectives. However, this requires significant expertise in sourcing deals, conducting due diligence, and managing portfolio companies, areas that demand substantial resources, deep industry knowledge, due diligence capabilities and robust risk management frameworks. Conversely, investing in an established private equity fund leverages the expertise, networks, and infrastructure of experienced managers, reducing the operational burden on the family office. While this provides diversification and professional oversight, it limits control and relies on the fund's diligence and risk management practices, which can vary widely. Family offices pursuing direct investments must build in-house expertise and systems to achieve desired growth and mitigate risks. In contrast, those opting to invest in funds must rigorously vet managers' track records, alignment of interests, and operational practices to ensure alignment with their Risk Tolerance and long-term goals.

Risk Landscape

These investments, however, come with inherent risks that require careful consideration, a few of which are further expounded upon below:

- **Illiquidity:** Private equity investments are typically illiquid, meaning they cannot be easily converted to cash. This illiquidity poses challenges if the family needs access to capital quickly or faces unforeseen financial emergencies.
- **Valuation Challenges:** Valuing private equity investments can be complex and subjective, particularly in the absence of readily

available market data. Accurate valuation is crucial for evaluating portfolio performance and making informed decisions, but it can be challenging.

- **Exit Strategy Risk:** In private equity this risk stems from the uncertainty of achieving a successful and profitable sale or liquidity event for a portfolio company. Challenges include market illiquidity, unforeseen company issues, and sale prices that are less than expected, all of which impact the timing and return on investment for private equity investors. Thorough planning and adaptability are crucial to mitigating this inherent risk.

- **Management Risk:** The success of a private equity investment heavily relies on the skill, competence and culture of the operating companies' management team, as well as that of the fund if opting for an indirect investment approach. Poor management can lead to significant losses, regardless of market conditions. Furthermore, a complete understanding of portfolio company and fund level succession planning, funding, and governance is critical.

- **Market Risk:** While often less susceptible to daily market fluctuations than publicly traded equities, private equity investments still face broader macroeconomic and market risks. Economic downturns, regulatory issues, or changes in industry dynamics can negatively affect performance.

- **Operational Risks:** Operational Risks present a particularly acute exposure for families investing directly in private companies or indirectly through private equity funds. Unlike publicly traded firms, where information is more standardized, disclosures more robust, and market pricing more transparent, private companies often operate with limited visibility, making it more difficult for families and advisors to assess the true depth of operational vulnerabilities.

Operational failures can arise from a wide range of factors: production bottlenecks, supply chain fragility, workforce shortages, regulatory violations, cybersecurity breaches, litigation, or breakdowns in management oversight. In direct investments, families may face these risks firsthand, sometimes with little diversification to soften the impact. In indirect investments, such as limited partnership commitments to private equity funds, these exposures are often embedded deep within the underlying portfolio companies, where investors have limited influence and must rely heavily on the general partner's competency, risk culture, and communication.

From a Total Family Balance Sheet Framework perspective, Operational Risk is not isolated, it can cascade across silos. For example, a family with substantial ownership in a manufacturing business through a private equity stake may also hold correlated exposures through supply chain dependent operating companies, industry specific real estate, or public equities tied to the same sector. A single operational failure can therefore create knock on effects that amplify financial, reputational, and liquidity strains across the family's broader holdings.

This highlights the importance of disciplined due diligence, stress testing, and ongoing monitoring, ensuring that private equity exposures are evaluated not only on potential return, but on the operational resilience of each underlying business, the quality of governance, and the alignment between the sponsor's risk practices and the family's long term objectives.

Due Diligence Challenges: Conducting thorough due diligence on private equity investments is crucial, but it can be particularly challenging due to the complexity of target companies, lack of regulatory oversight in private markets, and the limited information available.

Active vs. Passive Tax Liability Risk Tax

Tax implications differ significantly between active and passive private equity investments, and understanding these distinctions is crucial for managing risk across the Total Family Balance Sheet. Active investments where the family directly participates in the portfolio company's operations may allow certain tax deductions tied to management expenses, operational involvement, or business-related activities. However, they also expose the investor to a wider range of tax liabilities stemming from the company's day-to-day functions, including payroll taxes, sales taxes, excise taxes, and other obligations that flow through to owners depending on the entity structure.

By contrast, passive investments made through private equity funds generally utilize pass-through taxation. In these structures, the fund reports income, losses, deductions, and credits on a Schedule K-1, which is then passed directly to the investor's personal return. While this simplifies the fund's tax structure, it also limits the investor's ability to influence tax timing or plan proactively. The fund controls when gains are realized, when losses are harvested, and how income is characterized, whether as ordinary income, capital gains, or unrelated business taxable income (UBTI).

Importantly, in both active and passive structures, investors may incur taxable income without receiving a corresponding cash distribution.

This phenomenon, often referred to as "phantom income", occurs when a business or fund recognizes taxable profit on paper but elects to retain that profit for reinvestment, debt repayment, operational needs, or capital reserves. In an active investment, a family may face taxable income based on the entity's reported earnings even if the company distributes no cash due to expansion projects, working capital shortages, or unexpected operational expenses. In passive fund structures, a K-1 may reflect significant taxable profit from asset sales or mark-to-market adjustments without the fund making an actual distribution. In both scenarios, the family may be required to use outside liquidity, often from unrelated Asset Silos, to cover the tax liability created by the investment.

This risk underscores the importance of evaluating whether a private equity investment aligns with the family's broader liquidity strategy. Investments that produce taxable obligations without providing liquidity can strain cash flow, elevate reliance on other silos of the balance sheet, and increase the likelihood of making forced financial decisions under pressure.

The optimal approach therefore depends on individual circumstances, Risk Tolerance, and investment objectives. Families should collaborate with their CPA, tax strategist, and legal advisors to understand the tax dynamics of each investment structure, prepare for potential phantom income exposure, and integrate appropriate planning solutions. This ensures that decisions made in the private equity silo do not unintentionally create tax or liquidity shocks across the broader Total Family Balance Sheet.

Succession and Key Person Risk: Effective succession planning and key person protection are crucial for both individual direct private equity investments and a fund's overall stability. Within a single investment, the loss of key management or specialized expertise in the operating company due to unforeseen circumstances (such as resignation, death, disability, etc.) can severely impact the portfolio company's value and operational continuity, thereby jeopardizing the investor's return.

Figure 10.2 Exit Strategy + Key Person: How succession planning and key person risk may impact both portfolio companies and fund managers in private equity investments.

Board Seat Liability

Additional consideration should be given to individual family investments when a family member or one of their family office representatives serves on the board of a portfolio company. In these situations, the family is not only deploying financial capital but also leveraging its "Human Capital" the reputation, judgment, influence, and expertise of the individual serving. While board service can enhance a family's access to opportunities, information flow, and strategic influence, it simultaneously increases risk exposure because decisions made at the board level carry personal fiduciary responsibility. This means due diligence must be more thorough and ongoing, as the individual on the board can be held personally liable for breaches of duty, governance failures, or adverse outcomes stemming from board decisions.

Given these heightened exposures, families should ensure clarity around the portfolio company's transfer of such risks through appropriate professional liability coverage, including Errors and Omissions (E&O), Directors and Officers (D&O) insurance, and, where applicable, Representations and Warranties coverage. These structures help protect both the individual and the family's broader balance sheet from unintended consequences arising from board-level involvement.

Importantly, leveraging human capital in a portfolio company links this investment to other silos of the Total Family Balance Sheet, making risk interdependency more pronounced. A misstep at the board level can trigger cascading impact such as legal liability, reputational damage, financial strain, or strained family dynamics far beyond the initial investment. As with all other silos, these human capital risks should be evaluated through the four tools of risk management: Avoidance, Mitigation, Transference, or Assumption. The objective is to ensure that board participation is grounded in informed decision-making, robust protection strategies, and coordinated planning, rather than reactive or uninformed responses that could jeopardize multiple areas of the family's financial and personal life.

Fund Manager Succession Risk

At the fund level, the concentration of expertise and decision-making authority within a small group of key individuals, typically the fund managers, creates a material structural risk. Should one of these individuals retire, become disabled, depart unexpectedly, or pass away, the fund may face significant challenges in managing existing portfolio companies, sourcing and evaluating new opportunities, or executing its long-term strategy. For this reason, a core component of due diligence before making any fund-level investment should include a direct examination of the question: "What is the fund manager's succession plan?"

A clearly articulated and well-structured succession plan, that is funded while leveraging other risk-mitigation mechanisms, is essential for reducing this vulnerability. Such planning helps ensure operational continuity, protects the fund's strategic direction, and supports the long-term stability of the overall private equity allocation within the Total Family Balance Sheet.

Private Equity Operational Risk: Collapse of Toy Retailer

The collapse of a once-iconic toy retailer serves as a cautionary tale for investors in private equity funds, highlighting the importance of vetting a fund's risk management and due diligence processes, even when dealing with established firms. In 2005, three significant private equity firms acquired the iconic retailer in a $6.6 billion leveraged buyout, saddling it with considerable debt. Despite the company's strong brand recognition, the private equity owners failed to adapt the business to the rise of e-commerce and declining mall traffic, ultimately leading to its bankruptcy in 2017. For investors, this highlights the importance of carefully evaluating how private equity funds assess market trends, competition, and Operational Risks before investing. Key steps include reviewing the fund's historical performance, understanding its approach to industry analysis, and assessing whether its strategies prioritize sustainable growth over short-term financial engineering.

Figure 10.3: Systemic Risk in Private Equity: A cautionary tale of operational oversight, leverage, and transparency failures within a high-profile private equity-backed company.

Furthermore, investors should ensure that Private Equity funds have robust systems to mitigate risks, such as excessive leverage, and allocate sufficient capital for innovation and operational improvements. By demanding transparency and rigorous due diligence, investors can better insulate themselves from, and potentially avoid, exposure to flawed investments, even from the most reputable funds.

The Harsh Reality of Private Equity Investing

To focus on this, an exclusive risk management partner for a prominent angel private equity fund was entrusted with a dual role that highlighted the critical importance of risk management in the private equity fund's investment strategy. The Risk Manager's responsibilities included conducting comprehensive insurance reviews for their existing portfolio companies and evaluating coverage adequacy during the due diligence phase of new investments. During the Risk Managers' analysis, they uncovered a significant oversight: not one of the underlying investments had any insurance in place, and little-to-no risk management strategies, leaving the private equity firm and its portfolio companies highly exposed to potential liabilities. Despite highlighting this critical gap and the associated risks, the private equity fund ultimately chose not to act, prioritizing short-term financial metrics, such as EBITDA and return on investment, over long-term risk mitigation. The risk management firm ultimately severed its relationship with the private equity fund due to the potential for adverse legal events from fund investors, as it was most likely implied that with a dedicated Risk Manager and insurance partner, the underlying operating companies were adequately protected.

This example, along with that of the toy retailer, underscores a broader challenge within private equity, where the drive for immediate profitability can overshadow prudent risk management, potentially jeopardizing the stability and sustainability of investments. Private equity investing generally requires more up-front due diligence and risk management than any other silo. In most cases, when a family invests in Private Equity, they are placing significant trust in the fund or the underlying company's transparency and processes. Likely, the family is doing an adequate job of financial risk management but could be lacking in liability risk management finding and evaluating any off-balance-sheet exposures.

Checklist & Key Questions

By utilizing *The Total Family Balance Sheet by Higginbotham*™ checklist provided at the beginning of this chapter, a prudent Risk Manager can more comprehensively assess the risks associated with a family's holdings and how to develop a strategy for addressing these potentialities.

- Do I fully understand the liquidity risk of each private equity investment, including whether I could face taxable income without receiving a cash distribution, and how that strain would be funded across other silos of the Total Family Balance Sheet?
- Have I thoroughly evaluated the operational resilience of each underlying portfolio company, and do I know how a single

operational failure could cascade into correlated risks across my operating businesses, real estate, or investment portfolio?

- Do I have clear visibility into the fund manager's succession plan and key-person risk, and how would my investment be affected if a key decision-maker unexpectedly departed?
- If I or a family member sits on a portfolio company board, have we fully assessed the legal, reputational, and cross-silo consequences of that role, and confirmed that appropriate D&O, E&O, and related protections are in place?
- Have I critically evaluated each investment's exit strategy risk, specifically whether timing, market conditions, or leverage structures could delay or reduce returns at the very moment my family may require liquidity?
- Are we performing due diligence at a depth that ensures we are truly informed, not relying on assumptions, limited disclosures, or misplaced trust in fund managers or operating partners?

Conclusion
Integrating Private Equity into the Total Family Balance Sheet

Integrating private equity into the Total Family Balance Sheet requires more than a search for outsized returns; it demands a disciplined, cross-silo risk management mindset. By viewing each direct or fund investment through the lenses of liquidity, operational resilience, tax complexity (including the potential for phantom income), governance, succession, and human capital exposure, families can move from an Uninformed or Ill-Informed posture to one of intentional, eyes-wide-open decision-making.

Within this framework, private equity is no longer treated as a standalone "deal," but as one interdependent component of a broader ecosystem that includes operating businesses, real estate, investment portfolios, personal assets, and family human capital. Coordinated analysis among advisors (CPAs, legal counsel, investment professionals, and Risk Managers) enables families to identify where hidden Off-balance-sheet-liabilities may exist, how a single operational failure or board decision might cascade across silos, and whether the structure of a fund or company truly aligns with the family's long-term objectives and Risk Tolerance.

Ultimately, the Total Family Balance Sheet does not tell a family whether to pursue a particular private equity opportunity; rather, it equips them to consciously choose how to engage with it. Whether to Assume, Avoid, Mitigate, or Transfer the associated risks. When applied thoughtfully, this approach allows private equity to serve its intended role: a powerful engine for growth that is balanced by well-designed protections, supporting both wealth creation and preservation across generations instead of jeopardizing the very legacy it is meant to enhance.

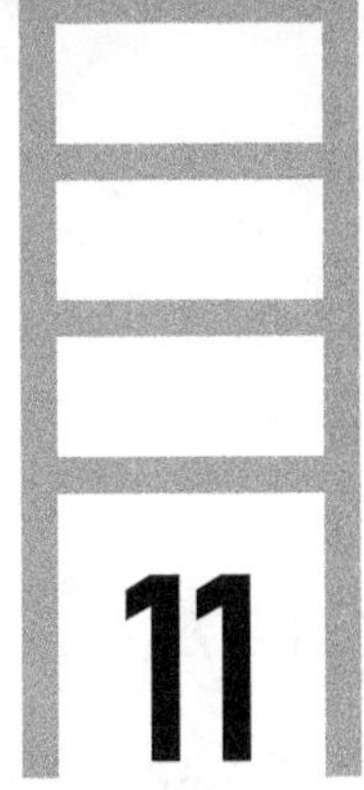

MANAGING RISK IN PERSONAL ASSETS
Toys, Treasures, and Trouble

While family-operating companies, investment portfolios, and real estate holdings often dominate discussions of wealth and risk management, successful individuals and families likely also possess significant personal assets such as homes, cars, boats, aircraft, toys, art, collectibles, jewelry, and other valuable items that require careful consideration. Frequently, these assets are overlooked because they are accumulated in small increments over a long period. A passionate collection of Goyard, Chanel, YSL, and Hermès apparel and accessory items can amass significant value. Still, they are often not considered in risk planning because individuals and families tend to view them as 'used.' They thus may have a consignment sale value, rather than their replacement value.

This chapter examines the distinct risks associated with these assets and outlines strategies for their effective management within the Total Family Balance Sheet framework.

Associated Risks	Informed	Uninformed	Avoid	Mitigate	Transfer	Assume
Aircraft	☐	☐	☐	☐	☐	☐
Audit/Legal	☐	☐	☐	☐	☐	☐
Auto	☐	☐	☐	☐	☐	☐
Benefits & EP Liability	☐	☐	☐	☐	☐	☐
Builders Risk	☐	☐	☐	☐	☐	☐
Collections	☐	☐	☐	☐	☐	☐
Cyber	☐	☐	☐	☐	☐	☐
Depreciation	☐	☐	☐	☐	☐	☐
Equip Breakdown	☐	☐	☐	☐	☐	☐
Estate	☐	☐	☐	☐	☐	☐
Flood	☐	☐	☐	☐	☐	☐
Fraud	☐	☐	☐	☐	☐	☐
General Liability	☐	☐	☐	☐	☐	☐
Libel and Slander	☐	☐	☐	☐	☐	☐
Loss of Use	☐	☐	☐	☐	☐	☐
Medical Expense	☐	☐	☐	☐	☐	☐
Non Profit D&O	☐	☐	☐	☐	☐	☐
Personal Injury	☐	☐	☐	☐	☐	☐
Political	☐	☐	☐	☐	☐	☐
Property	☐	☐	☐	☐	☐	☐
Regulatory	☐	☐	☐	☐	☐	☐
Reputation	☐	☐	☐	☐	☐	☐
Terrorism	☐	☐	☐	☐	☐	☐
Toys - ATV Golf Cart	☐	☐	☐	☐	☐	☐
Travel/Crisis/K&R	☐	☐	☐	☐	☐	☐
Watercraft	☐	☐	☐	☐	☐	☐
Workers' Compensation	☐	☐	☐	☐	☐	☐

Figure 11.1 Personal Assets: *A matrix illustrating how families can assess various personal asset-related risks ranging from aircraft to cyber threats and workers' compensation, etc. Viewing them across the spectrums of awareness (Informed vs. Uninformed) and the four tools of risk management: Avoidance, Mitigation, Transfer, or Assumption. This tool enables more intentional decision-making and prioritization of risk strategy for lifestyle assets within the Total Family Balance Sheet.*

The Hidden Vulnerabilities of Personal Assets

Personal assets, while often representing significant value and sentimental importance, are frequently overlooked in traditional risk management approaches. Usually, these assets can hold a different Emotional Risk Tolerance due to their potential for a long-term, deeply ingrained connection to the individual or family. Additionally, in many cases, personal assets are only second to the family-operating business in contributing to overall net worth, and are often neglected from a risk management standpoint. Frequently, a self-made family experiences rapid, significant increases in the value of their assets, but does not seek more sophisticated risk management advisors to meet the evolving needs that the new asset profile represents. Unlike family-operating businesses, which likely have enhanced their risk management strategies to address growth, families are more likely to stay with their previous advisors or turn to immediate, albeit often incomplete, solutions such as insurance from online portals or call centers. Too frequently, the risk management strategy for the family's personal assets is relegated to a last-minute decision without critical thought.

Often, risk management strategies are implemented after a new asset is acquired, which can potentially result in less-than-desirable risk management options, including the possibility that the asset could be uninsurable altogether. These last-minute decisions can frequently put far more than the value of the asset at risk, potentially exposing the family to Off-balance-sheet-liabilities, risking large portions of the overall family net worth.

Uninsurable Property After Purchase

For example, a family purchases a new property in Colorado, North Carolina, Texas, or California without consulting a property risk management professional before acquisition. After taking ownership, the family discovers that the wildfire risk is so immense that the property is uninsurable. Savvy families will frequently list their property in coastal or fire-prone areas for sale when the insurance becomes too expensive or unattainable, leaving the new family, who likely made an emotionally driven purchase decision, with a much larger liability than they anticipated.

Personal Negligence: The Modern Family's Biggest Exposure in the Era of Nuclear Verdicts and Litigation Finance

Personal liability has become one of the most consequential exposures facing individuals and families, particularly those with significant net worth. It encompasses the legal responsibility for one's actions or omissions, and in today's legal system, the financial consequences of even a single claim can be catastrophic. What was once a manageable risk has shifted dramatically due to two powerful accelerants: like the rise of **Nuclear Verdicts** and the rapid institutionalization of Litigation Finance.

Nuclear Verdicts, jury awards exceeding $10 million, are no longer rare outliers. Social Inflation, growing anti-wealth sentiment, evolving jury psychology, and increasingly sophisticated plaintiff tactics have fueled a legal environment where judgments can reach unprecedented levels. These outcomes are not limited to corporations; high net worth individuals and families are now routinely viewed as viable "deep pockets," making them prime targets for aggressive legal action.

Exacerbating this trend is the explosive growth of private-equity-backed litigation financing. Historically, the insurance company defending the accused was the party with the deepest pockets. Today, that dynamic has reversed. Litigation Finance firms, funded by institutional capital, now bankroll plaintiffs with virtually unlimited legal budgets. They treat lawsuits as a high-return asset class, financing expert testimony, expansive discovery, multi-year litigation campaigns, and sophisticated public-relations strategies engineered to maximize pressure and judgment size.

In many cases, the plaintiff's financial backers may now have more capital and greater staying power than the defendant's insurance carrier. Plaintiffs no longer face the financial constraints that once encouraged settlement. Instead, litigation financiers empower them to pursue the largest possible judgment, knowing investors, not plaintiffs, shoulder the risk and stand to profit from an outsized verdict.

Against this backdrop, merely "having insurance" is no longer sufficient. The structure of liability coverage, particularly how defense costs are handled, now plays a central role in whether a family is protected or dangerously exposed. A well-designed liability program can be the difference between absorbing a lawsuit and experiencing catastrophic financial loss.

As **Nuclear Verdicts** expand and litigation financing grows more aggressive, families must reassess personal liability risk with modern realities in mind. Strong legal structuring, robust excess liability programs, thoughtful personal behavior, and guidance from experienced advisors have become essential components of a contemporary personal risk strategy.

Risk Planning for Personal Assets: How Modern Liability Insurance Really Works

Individuals and families must apply the four tools of risk management, Avoidance, Mitigation, Transference, or Assumption, to their personal assets just as they would with a family business. Unfortunately, many continue to make incomplete or rushed asset protection decisions without integrating their personal risks into a cohesive framework.

A holistic strategy often includes proper legal structuring (Family Limited Partnerships, Trusts, LLCs, and other entities), the use of creditor protected financial vehicles (such as 401(k)s, 409A plans, and certain defined benefit or deferred compensation structures), and tools like life insurance and annuities that carry statutory protection in many jurisdictions. Together, these components create layered defenses against litigation, liability, and creditor claims.

Yet even with sophisticated structuring, liability insurance contracts remain the backbone of risk transfer, and few families fully understand the mechanics of what they are actually buying. In particular, the distinction between the duty to defend and the duty to indemnify is one of the most misunderstood (and most consequential) aspects of any insurance policy.

The Critical Distinction: Duty to Defend vs. Duty to Indemnify

Duty to Defend Equals Insurer Controls the Fight

Under most liability policies, the insurer has the contractual obligation to take control of the policyholder's defense once a claim is filed. This means the insurer, not the policyholder, decides which attorneys will represent you, how the legal strategy will unfold, how aggressively to fight, when to settle, and what settlement amount is acceptable.

By tendering a claim, the policyholder effectively transfers their right to decide and their right to direct their own defense. In exchange, the insurer assumes the cost of legal representation.

This arrangement is beneficial in many cases, but in high-profile or complex matters, it can place the insurer's interests and the family's interests at odds. Sophisticated families must understand the implications of this transfer of control and purchase the policy with the most favorable contract language, not that with the lowest price.

Duty to Indemnify Equals Insurer Agrees to Pay for the Outcome

This is the insurer's obligation to pay settlements or judgments, but only after the defense is complete and only up to the policy's stated limit.

Defense Inside vs. Outside the Policy Limit: The Difference Between Protection and Disaster

Whether defense costs are "inside" or "outside" the liability limit materially changes the potential value of the coverage:

Defense Inside the Limit

Legal defense costs reduce the policy's total limit available for settlement or judgment. In a world where defense expenses routinely reach millions, a policy's limit can evaporate long before a case is resolved.

Defense Outside the Limit

Defense costs are paid separately by the insurer and do not erode the liability limit. This preserves the full limit for indemnity and provides significantly greater protection against prolonged, well-funded litigation campaigns.

The difference between these two structures often determines whether a family's assets remain safe, or dangerously exposed.

Why Umbrella & Excess Policies Matter More Than Ever

Umbrella and excess liability contracts remain one of the most cost-effective tools available for transferring catastrophic personal liability risk. These policies sit above home, auto, and other primary coverages, providing a critical layer of additional protection in a world defined by Nuclear Verdicts and Litigation Finance. Just as importantly, they increase the insurer's own financial exposure, often meaning the carrier has stronger motivation to mount a high-quality, well-resourced defense on the policyholder's behalf.

When insurers face greater potential loss, they tend to assign more seasoned claims professionals, retain higher tier legal counsel, and pursue more strategic, proactive litigation defenses. For high net worth families who may become targets of sophisticated plaintiff strategies, this alignment of financial interests offers a powerful, often underappreciated advantage.

Figure 11.2 Umbrella Policy + Burglars: *A visual overview of how excess liability (umbrella) insurance can help shield personal assets from catastrophic claims arising from negligence or liability exposure due to a 'burglar' aka nuclear verdict stealing personal assets.*

The Importance of Asset Structuring

Consider a family who purchases a car for their adult son, who is going through a difficult period, perhaps a recent divorce, job loss, or other personal setback. Wanting to help, the parents buy the vehicle to support him. However, either out of concern that he might sell the car or simply out of lack of awareness, they title the vehicle in their own names. Unbeknownst to them, liability follows the titled owner.

Months later, the son begins engaging in illegal street racing, proudly posting videos and results on social media, posts in which his father is clearly tagged and visible. One night, disaster strikes: during a race, the son is involved in a catastrophic accident that kills him and two innocent bystanders. Believing their personal insurance will protect them, the parents are initially unaware of the magnitude of the exposure they now face.

The families of the two victims file a lawsuit against the parents, asserting contributory and gross negligence for providing and maintaining ownership of the vehicle. The plaintiffs seek $5 million in damages and ultimately prevail. Worse still, because the verdict includes gross negligence, the court allows punitive (or "exemplary") damages, doubling the award to $10 million. In some states, this multiplier can even reach three times the judgment or have no statutory cap.

The parents, already devastated by the loss of their son, are now forced to endure years of legal proceedings and face a massive financial judgment, one that reaches into their personal net worth simply because the vehicle was titled in their names.

This outcome could have been entirely avoided with basic risk-aware structuring. The parents could have titled the car directly in their son's name, cleanly separating liability from their personal assets. If they were worried he might sell the car, they could have listed themselves as lienholders while keeping the title in his name. Either approach would have walled off liability and protected their broader balance sheet. Additional options, such as owning the vehicle through an LLC, can also provide effective risk isolation for higher-exposure families.

It's true that transferring ownership or using an entity might increase insurance costs, particularly with a youthful driver. But the real comparison is not the 10–15% increase in premiums, it's the multimillion-dollar exposure that results from failing to structure assets properly.

An umbrella and/or excess policy might have provided meaningful protection as well, potentially covering most or all the damages. However, many insurance policies exclude punitive damages. This reinforces the need to apply the full set of risk management tools, Avoidance, Mitigation, Transference, or Assumption and to understand both the benefits and limitations of the insurance contracts being purchased.

Proper structuring, paired with thoughtful insurance design, may help prevent a tragic situation from becoming a financial catastrophe.

Valuation, Vulnerability, and Coverage Gaps in Personal Holdings

Personal assets frequently have several additional challenges that are unique versus the other Asset Silos covered in The Total Family Balance Sheet.

Accurately valuing personal assets can be complex and subjective, especially for items lacking readily available market data (e.g., unique art pieces, collections, antique furniture). Proper valuation is crucial for insurance purposes, estate planning, and overall financial assessment.

Personal assets are also more frequently vulnerable to theft, loss, and damage from various sources, including burglary, internal or domestic employee theft, cyber theft, fire, natural disasters, and accidental damage.

Traditional homeowner's, property, and auto insurance policies may not provide adequate coverage for high-value personal assets. Specialized insurance may be necessary to cover losses fully. Due to the complexity of insurance contracts and the specificity required to transfer risk adequately, insurance often presents its challenges, some of which are highlighted below and warrant further exploration. The challenges typically arise from a family being Ill-Informed or Uninformed about the risks and the correct use of the four tools of risk management; Avoidance, Mitigation, Transference, and Assumption

Lessons from Wildfire and Hurricane Losses: Preparing Before It's Too Late

After major hurricanes and wildfires, countless property owners discover a painful truth: their homes, real estate holdings, and even businesses were severely underinsured. Only when the catastrophe has already occurred do they learn that their coverage, often based on outdated valuations, falls far short of the actual cost to rebuild.

This was clearly seen after Hurricane Harvey in 2017, when many Texas homeowners learned that soaring construction and labor costs had raced far ahead of the limits on their policies. The same pattern followed the 2018 and 2025 California wildfires, where widespread destruction collided with dramatically higher rebuilding costs. Families who believed they were "fully covered" often found themselves hundreds of thousands, or even millions, of dollars short.

A major contributor is the age of many impacted properties. Homes built decades earlier were constructed under simpler, cheaper building codes, codes that may no longer exist. When these structures are destroyed, they must be rebuilt to modern standards. Updated codes, stricter permitting requirements, inflation, labor shortages, and environmental regulations all combine to make reconstruction far more expensive than owners realize. As a result, only a fraction of homes lost to catastrophic events are rebuilt within a decade; many are never rebuilt at all.

When Homes Can't Be Rebuilt:
Lessons from Santa Barbara, CA

Santa Barbara offers a stark example. Following the devastating wildfires and mudslides of 2018, entire neighborhoods were wiped out. Nearly ten years later, only a small percentage of those homes have been rebuilt. Many homeowners discovered too late that their coverage limits did not account for modern building codes, significant increases in labor and materials, or newly imposed construction regulations. What they thought would be a manageable process quickly became financially impossible.

These examples underscore the importance of regular insurance reviews, especially for properties in high-risk areas such as California, Texas, Colorado, Louisiana, and Florida. In these regions, some affluent homeowners choose to forgo insurance entirely because premiums have become so expensive. While this may seem financially appealing in the short term, it exposes families to losses that can permanently destabilize their entire balance sheet.

Lack of Proper Inventorying Before a Loss

A common misconception in property and casualty insurance is that the insurance carrier must prove what was lost. In reality, the burden of proof falls entirely on the insured. After a loss, the policyholder must demonstrate that they owned the item, that the item was present at the property, the quality and condition of the item, and the value of the item.

This contrasts sharply with life insurance, where the policyholder and insured must prove insurable interest and insurability before the contract is issued. Property insurance, by comparison, is easy to obtain, but much harder to collect on without proper documentation, whereas life insurance is typically more difficult to obtain but seen as easier to collect on because all that is typically required is a Certificate of Death.

"My proof burned down with the house."

This phrase is tragically common after disasters. Without proper inventorying, families struggle to reconstruct what they owned, down to appliances, furniture, art, jewelry, equipment, collections, and even the materials used inside the home. Insurers typically require photos, serial numbers, appraisals, receipts, or other proof before paying a claim.

While businesses routinely track their assets on a schedule (e.g., steel in the warehouse, computers in a server room, furniture on a depreciation schedule) and have redundancy of those documents (i.e., backed up in the cloud or copies with their Risk Manager or attorney), families rarely apply the same discipline at home. If they do, often they keep the schedule of assets in the home itself without redundancy, susceptible to the same damage as the assets. As a result, after a fire or flood, they are left trying to recall years' worth of purchases from memory, often while under extreme emotional stress. The outcome is predictable: items go undocumented, claims are reduced or denied, and families find themselves unexpectedly self-insuring large portions of their loss.

Underinsurance by Choice: A Preventable Mistake

When determining how much risk to transfer through an insurance policy, families must weigh both cost and consequence. A common, and dangerous mistake is choosing insufficient coverage simply because the premium for full reconstruction cost feels too high. Some families opt for lower limits or even partial self-insurance, believing they are saving money. In reality, they are exposing themselves to the potentially overwhelming effects of Financial Gravity.

A relatable tale comes from known personalities who proudly declare they "self-insure" their multimillion-dollar homes. Yet many may be far better off fully insuring a $5 million home with a $1 million deductible and acquiring named-peril or catastrophic coverage. While they would be responsible for the first $1 million after a disaster, the policy would still protect them from the remaining $4 million of loss, coverage that often can make the difference between rebuilding and financial ruin.

Understanding the Difference:
High-Frequency vs. High-Severity Risk

One of the most common mistakes families make when considering self-insurance is misunderstanding which risks they can safely absorb and which risks can financially destroy them. People often focus on the wrong category, worrying about small, frequent losses while overlooking the rare but catastrophic events that can cause complete financial collapse.

As discussed before, actuarial science, and a core philosophy of the Total Family Balance Sheet Framework, makes an important distinction between High Frequency / Low Severity risks and those that are Low Frequency / High Severity.

High Frequency / Low Severity risks (e.g., minor auto damage, small household repairs)

These happen often but cost relatively little. These are the kinds of risks that can be reasonably self-insured without threatening long-term stability.

Low Frequency / High Severity risks (e.g., a home burning down, a total-loss hurricane event)

These events are rare, but when they occur, the financial impact can be devastating. These risks should almost always be transferred through insurance or other contractual mechanisms.

A more effective strategy than dropping coverage is to carry strong protection for catastrophic losses potentially while using higher deductibles or self-insured retentions to reduce costs. This may help keep premiums more manageable without exposing the family to devastating loss.

Sophisticated families and advisors understand this balance. They evaluate all options, including catastrophic "**Named-Peril**" coverages, which provide targeted protection likely at a fraction of the cost of broad "All-Risk" policies.

Self-insuring can be appropriate, but only when it matches both a family's Emotional Risk Tolerance and Physical (financial) Risk Tolerance.

Unfortunately, many families make decisions based on frustration over rising premiums rather than a clear understanding of the financial consequences of a total loss. Without proper analysis, they may unknowingly assume risks that could jeopardize their entire financial foundation.

The Danger of Emotion-Driven Decisions

This pattern is frequently visible after disasters, when uninsured or underinsured public figures appear on national media seeking sympathy, and blaming insurers or policymakers for losses that were ultimately the result of their own risk decisions. Emotional responses cannot replace thoughtful planning.

Working with an experienced Risk Manager may help families strike the right balance between cost, coverage, and long-term protection, bridging the gap between fear-based reactions and sound financial decision-making.

Where Families Get It Right, and Where They Don't

Interestingly, most successful families are highly disciplined in other areas of their Total Family Balance Sheet. They make thoughtful, data-driven decisions in their real estate holdings and family operating businesses, supported by trusted legal, tax, and financial advisors.

Yet this same level of rigor is often missing in the personal Asset Silo.

Personal assets, homes, collections, vehicles, aircraft, and valuables, are frequently where families make rushed decisions, neglect to update valuations, or rely on outdated assumptions. This disconnect creates one of the most significant liability and property risk exposures to the family's wealth.

By bringing the same level of professional oversight and intentional planning to personal assets as they do to their operating businesses, families can better reduce preventable losses and strengthen their overall risk posture.

Beyond insurance decisions and structuring strategies, families can strengthen the protection of their personal assets through a range of practical Avoidance, Mitigation, Tranference, and Assumption techniques. These complementary practices help preserve both the financial and intrinsic value of personal property, reducing the likelihood of loss while enhancing resilience when unforeseen events occur. From improving physical security and storage conditions to maintaining proper legal structures, obtaining specialized insurance, and guarding against fraud in high-value markets, each approach plays a meaningful role in creating a comprehensive and intentional personal asset risk management strategy. The following examples highlight several of these tools and illustrate how they can be applied in everyday decision-making to safeguard a family's most cherished possessions.

Figure 11.3 High Security Vault: A depiction of best practices for securing and preserving high-value personal assets, from physical protection (vaults, alarms) to legal structuring and insurance.

- **Storage and Security:** Secure storage and adequate security measures are crucial for safeguarding valuable items against theft and damage. This extends beyond simple home security to potentially include long-term backup power sources, climate-controlled storage facilities, or high-security vaults, as well as off-site or cloud-based digital storage for essential documents.
- **Specialized Insurance:** Obtaining appropriate insurance coverage tailored to specific assets, including fine art insurance, jewelry insurance, and other specialized policies, is crucial for protecting against loss or damage.

- **Preservation and Maintenance:** Some personal assets (e.g., art, antiques) require specialized conservation and maintenance to ensure their long-term value and condition. This can include professional cleaning, restoration, and the implementation of appropriate environmental controls.

- **Legal Structuring:** Structuring personal assets in trusts or legal entities, such as LLCs, is an effective way to protect wealth from liability claims. By transferring assets into a trust or LLC, individuals separate their holdings from direct ownership, shielding them from creditors or lawsuits. Trusts offer additional privacy, control, and flexibility in asset management. Working with a qualified Risk Manager who collaborates with relevant legal and financial advisors helps ensure these structures comply with applicable laws and align with long-term wealth protection goals, providing a powerful tool to mitigate risk and safeguard personal assets.

- **Fraud Risk:** The market for rare and collectible items, including fine wines, art, and vintage watches, is becoming increasingly attractive to investors and collectors. However, with high-value items comes the significant risk of fraud, as many of these objects are difficult to verify for authenticity. Well-publicized legal battles over counterfeit wines highlighted just one example of this challenge, with rare bottles being sold as prestigious vintages despite being fake. Similar issues exist in the art market, where forgeries can be expertly crafted and pass through auction houses or galleries undetected. Vintage watches, often bought for their rarity and investment potential, can also fall victim to counterfeiters who replicate every detail to the untrained eye. As the market for these collectibles grows, the need for expert authentication, clear provenance, and rigorous due diligence becomes paramount to protect investors from financial losses. In these markets, where items are often one-of-a-kind, the risk of fraud is compounded, making authenticity verification a critical factor for anyone seeking to preserve the value of their collections.

Where Lifestyle Meets Risk

Many successful families have moved from commercial air travel to private air travel. While this often represents achieving a certain level of success in life, it also brings with it new potential for significant liability. As expected, aircraft represent significant potential liability due to the complexity of the business and the physical cost of the assets.

Whether a family is purchasing an aircraft in its entirety, a fractional share, a 'jet' card, or chartering individual flights, the potential liability exposure is often real and significant. Depending on how the family engages in this market, there should always be an aircraft attorney, and a competent Risk Manager involved in the transaction.

Jet Charter with Lithium Battery Fire

To highlight this, a family who purchases a fractional interest and/or jet card with a well-established national provider may be surprised to be told that the standard 'non-negotiated' language is typically favored for the writer of the contract. This can result in a potentially significant imbalance in the responsibility of liability exposure between the consumer and the provider.

For example, who is responsible for the damage to the aircraft if you, as the passenger or one of your guests, are responsible for causing a fire in the cargo hold of the plane, such as when a lithium-ion battery catches fire during your use of the aircraft?

Consumers often don't realize that the person who started the chain reaction of events is where negligence (and hence liability) falls. In the fire example above, the consumer's battery caused damage to the plane, injuries to the passengers, pilots, and bystanders, as well as loss of income to the provider due to the plane being out of commission for repairs. Furthermore, there is a risk to the diminished value of the aircraft, as the logbooks now reflect an accident or damage repair history. All costs associated with this fire may be borne by the person who chartered the plane.

This can be rectified by two of the tools of risk management, mitigation and transference. First, in a mitigation strategy, the provider can change the indemnity language of the contract to remove liability from the consumer for any actions. If this is not an option or the provider is unwilling to do so, the consumer could also ask the provider to add their name as an additional insured to the provider's aircraft insurance. Or, in the worst (and often most financially expensive) case, the consumer could always purchase an independent, non-owned aircraft insurance policy.

Often as a family finds more financial success their desires for a more luxury lifestyle follow shortly thereafter. This can be seen through activities such as renting luxury estates, chartering yachts, taking extensive vacations, and/or the use of private aircraft. All of these activities have similar exposures as outlined above with the lithium battery example and should be accounted for in the family's risk management strategy.

Checklist & Key Questions

- Are our homes and high-value properties insured to **true reconstruction cost**, not purchase price, tax value, or market value, and reviewed regularly for inflation and updated building code requirements?
- Do we carry enough umbrella and excess liability insurance, with **defense costs outside the limit**, to protect our net worth in a world of Nuclear Verdicts and litigation financed lawsuits?
- Are personal assets, especially homes, vehicles, collections, and lifestyle assets, titled or structured correctly (e.g., LLCs, trusts, lienholder arrangements) to isolate liability from the family's broader balance sheet?
- Do we maintain proper documentation, photos, serial numbers, and appraisals (stored off-site or in the cloud) so we can **prove** ownership, quality, and value after a fire, theft, or disaster?
- When we self-insure or under-insure, are we doing so only for **high-frequency/low-severity** risks, while transferring **low-frequency/high-severity** risks that could cause financial ruin?

- Do we fully understand where liability falls when using lifestyle assets (chartered aircraft, yachts, rentals, guest drivers) and do we carry non-owned coverage when appropriate?

Conclusion
Integrating Personal Assets into the Total Family Balance Sheet Framework

Personal assets, homes, collections, vehicles, aircraft, luxury items, and lifestyle experiences, may seem secondary compared to operating companies or investment portfolios, but as this chapter illustrates, they often present some of the most significant and misunderstood risks within a family's Total Family Balance Sheet. These assets grow quietly over time, accumulate emotional meaning, and frequently escape the rigorous oversight families apply to their business or financial holdings. Yet their exposure to natural disasters, theft, liability, litigation, valuation errors, structuring mistakes, and modern legal trends like Nuclear Verdicts and Litigation Finance can create vulnerabilities capable of destabilizing even the most carefully built fortune.

By adopting the same intentional planning, disciplined risk assessment, and professional advisory support used in other silos of the balance sheet, families can transform this historically overlooked area into one of strength and resilience. Through proper asset structuring, comprehensive documentation, thoughtful insurance design, and strategic use of the four tools of risk management, Avoidance, Mitigation, Transference, or Assumption, families can help protect not only the financial value of their personal assets but also the lifestyle, legacy, and emotional well-being these possessions represent. Ultimately, managing personal assets with clarity and foresight is not merely about preventing loss, it is about safeguarding the family's stability and ensuring that the forces of Financial Gravity do not erode the wealth they have worked so hard to build.

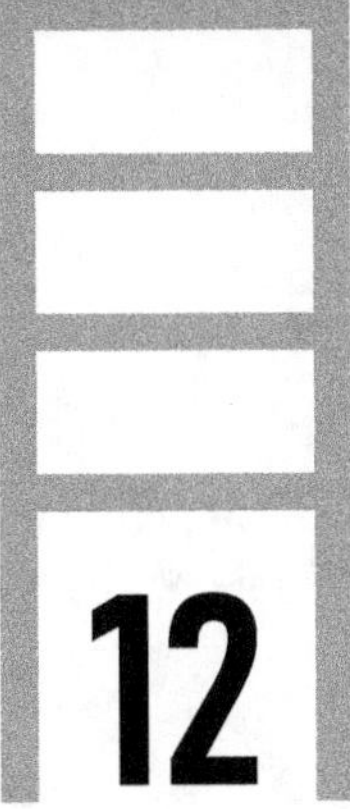

12

FAMILY HUMAN CAPITAL

The Intangible Asset

While financial assets, such as investments and real estate, are easily quantifiable, the Total Family Balance Sheet Framework acknowledges the profound, sometimes intangible, value of family human capital. This encompasses the collective skills, knowledge, relationships, family name, reputation, and networks within the family, assets that significantly enhance the family's overall well-being and potential for long-term success. This chapter examines the importance of evaluating and cultivating this crucial, yet often overlooked, asset class, which is arguably the most valuable.

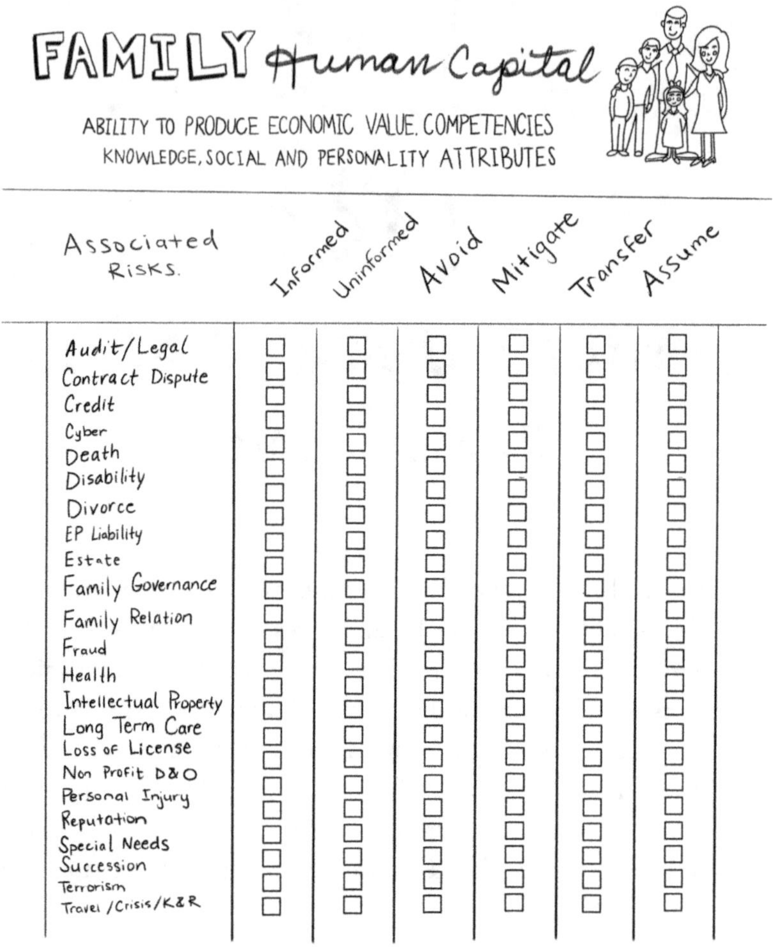

Associated Risks.	Informed	Uninformed	Avoid	Mitigate	Transfer	Assume
Audit/Legal	☐	☐	☐	☐	☐	☐
Contract Dispute	☐	☐	☐	☐	☐	☐
Credit	☐	☐	☐	☐	☐	☐
Cyber	☐	☐	☐	☐	☐	☐
Death	☐	☐	☐	☐	☐	☐
Disability	☐	☐	☐	☐	☐	☐
Divorce	☐	☐	☐	☐	☐	☐
EP Liability	☐	☐	☐	☐	☐	☐
Estate	☐	☐	☐	☐	☐	☐
Family Governance	☐	☐	☐	☐	☐	☐
Family Relation	☐	☐	☐	☐	☐	☐
Fraud	☐	☐	☐	☐	☐	☐
Health	☐	☐	☐	☐	☐	☐
Intellectual Property	☐	☐	☐	☐	☐	☐
Long Term Care	☐	☐	☐	☐	☐	☐
Loss of License	☐	☐	☐	☐	☐	☐
Non Profit D&O	☐	☐	☐	☐	☐	☐
Personal Injury	☐	☐	☐	☐	☐	☐
Reputation	☐	☐	☐	☐	☐	☐
Special Needs	☐	☐	☐	☐	☐	☐
Succession	☐	☐	☐	☐	☐	☐
Terrorism	☐	☐	☐	☐	☐	☐
Travel /Crisis/K&R	☐	☐	☐	☐	☐	☐

Figure 12.1 A more complete overview of how a prudent Risk Manager would consider the risks associated with Family Human Capital and how to consider building a strategy for addressing those potentialities.

Risk Landscape

Family Human Capital is the asset class most susceptible to the effects of Financial Gravity. The "shirtsleeve-to-shirtsleeve" analogy discussed in earlier chapters often stems from the consequences of poorly managed Family Human Capital. This concept suggests that wealth can diminish over time when family assets are ineffectively distributed and/or not nurtured for growth, in contrast to the opportunities that arise with adequate governance maintained across generations.

Building on previous discussions about the Forbes 400, we can see how Financial Gravity can impact a family's ability to sustain wealth and achieve ongoing economic growth and family harmony. Families that approach their estates with the same rigor as a business owner manages succession planning are typically better positioned for enduring success. Those who have navigated the challenges of time often run their Family Human Capital like a business, relying on robust Family Governance, trusted advisors, and consistent execution of those governance plans over many years.

Several factors come into play when considering Family Human Capital and the necessity of Family Governance. Wealth is often created by just one or two generations, and without innovation and proactive management, it can dissipate rapidly in response to changing markets, distribution demands from the family, and inadequate risk management.

Taxicab vs. Rideshare Market Shift

For instance, a family with a successful taxicab business may face declining revenue as the ride-sharing industry gains traction. A savvy family would either sell the company at its peak, adapt its operations to participate in the ride-sharing economy, or utilize its value to diversify into other asset classes, thereby safeguarding against market shifts. As time progresses, family businesses must navigate numerous challenges, some of which are potentially catastrophic to the family's net worth. Furthermore, the family estate may need to provide financial support to an expanding number of descendants. If it fails to diversify away from a limited number of core assets, it may struggle to meet the increased demands of new family members and their financial obligations.

Successful families often implement stringent corporate governance, combined with wealth preservation and growth strategies, that fairly compensate their most productive members at rates equal to those of non-family employees in the market. This frequently coincides with a linear distribution model, where each generation receives a fraction of the estate value (e.g., Generation 1 receives X, Generation 2 receives X-1, and so forth). Research indicates that families intent on perpetuating wealth typically distribute no more than 4% of the estate's value annually, based on financial performance. Importantly, effective Family Governance prevents immediate wealth dissipation to heirs upon the passing of a family member; instead, it emphasizes allowing Asset Silos to be managed and optimized together (i.e., the whole estate) to compound on a larger principal amount without erosion. While it may take a family 75 years to build its assets to a $1 billion value, they can frequently double to $2 billion in as little as 5-7 years, or they can lose it entirely within the same timeframe.

Family Distribution Erosion

We have observed instances where substantial estates are distributed, resulting in one heir thriving while another struggles. Beyond the potential financial ramifications and wealth erosion, this can create significant rifts within families, with some branches flourishing while others fight for survival. Conversely, a wealth-preservation approach compensates diligent and talented family members through operating salaries and financial incentives, alongside their lineal distributions, rewarding hard work and family lineage while mitigating the risks associated with Financial Gravity.

Designing Modern Family Governance: Where Structure Meets Culture

Modern family governance planning is increasingly attuned to these complex dynamics and is executed just as a complex business. So many times, the term family governance is construed to mean dictators, issues decrees from high, strict monarchy, or 'dictating from the grave.' The truth is, modern Family Governance is similar to modern corporate governance; there are two facets to it: Family Financial Governance, which encompasses the legal structuring as well as the management of business and investment assets. Family Emotional Governance, or 'Culture,' serves as the moral compass of the estate, enabling dynamic changes in Family

Financial Governance over time. Great families and great companies have a noble business model with a purpose, a promise, a mission, and a vision.

The Family Emotional Governance is in place to help maintain that noble business model throughout the generations. Through engaging expert legal, tax, risk management, and wealth management professionals, families can be best positioned to create a Family Financial and Emotional Governance plan that guides them over a long period by aligning their strategies with the original intentions of their founders, focusing on long-term wealth preservation and growth. Families that embrace these principles are often able to mitigate the effects of Financial Gravity, allowing their wealth to accumulate at an impressive rate and enabling them to rise in prominence, potentially earning a spot among the ranks of the Forbes 400 rather than plummeting like a meteor.

Financial Gravity & the Forbes 400

It is crucial to emphasize that the nearly 383 families on the original Forbes 400 list believed themselves insulated from the consequences of Financial Gravity due to their extraordinary asset accumulation. Financial Gravity has the same downward pressure on all estates. Those that are smaller (or closer to the surface) have less cushion to insulate themselves from meteoric surface impact, whereas a much larger estate can withstand Financial Gravity for longer. While the larger estate can suffer a much greater loss, the potential loss from a purely dollar-based perspective will likely be much greater than for the family with fewer assets. In reality, the less wealth you have, the harder it is to maintain, transfer, and grow generational wealth. It's exponentially harder. That said, ironically, even the most affluent families can be particularly at risk, often lulled into a false sense of security by their success.

Beyond Financial Assets: The Value of Human Capital

Family human capital encompasses far more than financial resources; it includes the skills, experience, values, and relationships that fuel long-term success across generations. This form of capital is built through specialized professional expertise, entrepreneurial instincts, management capability, technical proficiency, and intellectual property, ranging from patents to proprietary processes and other knowledge-based assets. Together, these attributes strengthen the family's overall financial engine and create a foundation for sustained prosperity.

Education and professional development play a central role in this process, enhancing a family member's earning potential and preparing them to contribute meaningfully to the family enterprise. Yet human capital is not limited to what individuals know or what they can do. It also reflects the opportunities naturally afforded to descendants of successful families, including access to elite schools, exclusive social and professional networks, unique investment opportunities, and influential circles that compound advantages over time. These forms of access, rooted in legacy, reputation, and social capital, can meaningfully elevate or erode the family's long-term prosperity depending on how they are cultivated and transferred.

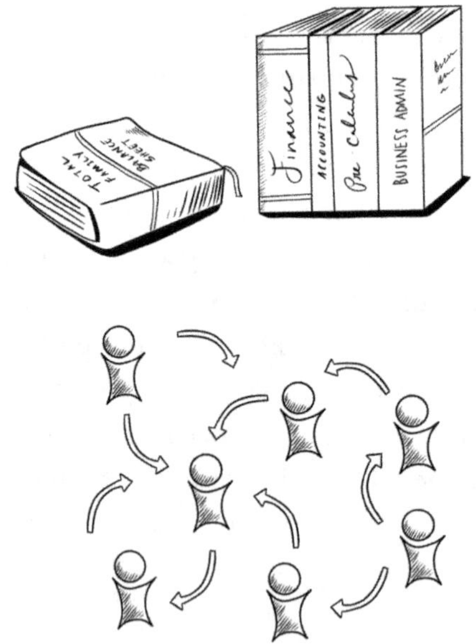

Figure 12.3 Education + Networking: Education and access are cornerstones of Family Human Capital. This visual underscores how family legacy, mentorship, social capital, and institutional access compound generational wealth. These intangible assets can either elevate or erode a family's long-term prosperity, depending on how they are cultivated and transferred.

A family's network of relationships is equally valuable. Personal and professional connections built over decades open doors to opportunities in business, philanthropy, education, and leadership. Research consistently shows that descendants of high-net-worth families enjoy a markedly higher likelihood of success, partly due to the strength and depth of these inherited networks. Active engagement within the family's ecosystem strengthens these connections across generations, ensuring that knowledge, mentorship, and relationships are continually renewed.

Human capital also includes the family's ability to govern itself well. The capacity to make sound decisions, manage conflict constructively, communicate effectively, articulate shared values, and adapt to changing environments directly influences family cohesion and long-term financial stability. Strong governance structures provide clarity around decision-making, create forums for communication, and establish mechanisms for resolving disputes, all of which enhance the sustainability of both wealth and relationships.

Nurturing this form of capital requires intentional, long-term strategy. Succession planning helps ensure the seamless transition of knowledge, capabilities, and leadership responsibilities from one generation to the next. Mentorship programs, both formal and informal, transfer wisdom, experience, and technical skills that might otherwise be lost. Investments in education and professional training develop the next generation's capabilities and earning potential. Regular family meetings and governance processes help maintain alignment, reinforce shared values, and provide structure for collaborative decision-making. Strong relationships within the family cultivate emotional resilience and strengthen the family's collective sense of identity and purpose. Finally, encouraging community engagement and participation in broader professional networks broadens access to resources and opportunities that support continued growth and protection.

Thoughtful planning for the transition of all asset classes, including family human capital, is essential within the Total Family Balance Sheet. Well-designed inheritance structures reduce conflict, ensure smoother generational transitions, and, when paired with effective wealth-transfer tax planning, meaningfully increase the net assets and advantages transferred to future generations. In this way, human capital becomes the connective tissue that binds a family's wealth, values, and legacy together. When cultivated intentionally, it is the asset most capable of outlasting markets, business cycles, and even financial capital itself.

The Most Predictable Risks Are the Most Ignored

There are countless examples of how not adequately addressing this silo can cause significant problems, because it is often overlooked. Recall the 'foundational risk focus' discussion in Chapter 1. If you are going to manage risk from a foundational perspective, death would be the number one problem to solve for, cybersecurity would be number two. Both are often virtually always overlooked or not adequately planned for.

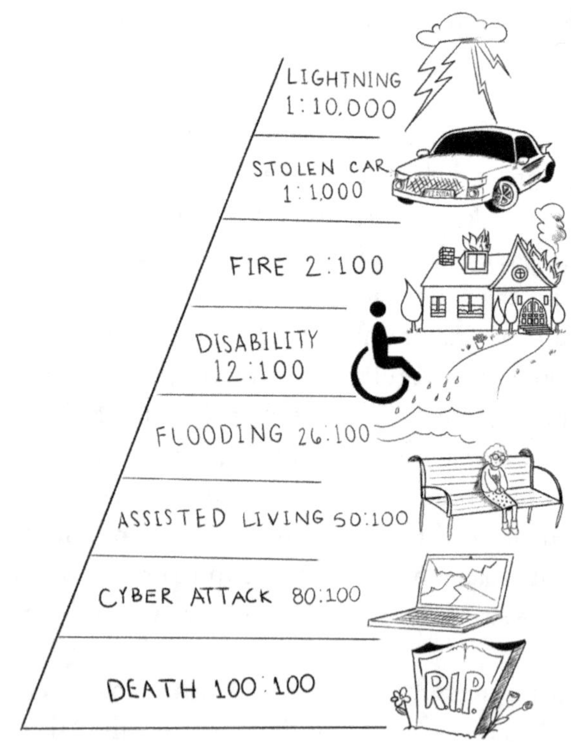

Figure 12.4 Foundational Risk Prioritization: *Focus risk strategy on events most likely and most damaging.*

Starting with the second most likely risk in all our lives, often a family does little to no risk management work for their IT network infrastructure in their personal life, including homes, yachts, and planes. Frequently, allowing an off-the-shelf, inexpensive router or other hardware devices with no encryption or other firewall protection. At the same time, the family is conducting increasing amounts of business from these locations, and their personal lives are being broadcast across these unsecured networks. Cybersecurity is becoming an increasingly vulnerable area; a simple internet search reveals that 8 in 10 people will experience a security breach during their lifetime. A breach can very quickly leave a family's most private secrets open to blackmail or other criminal activity. If a family took the same approach to their personal cybersecurity as they do to their business cybersecurity, this risk can be virtually mitigated entirely for an immaterial expense. Furthermore, if the family-operating business provides this structure, because work is conducted from home, the cost is often considered a legitimate business expense.

The number one risk, the only probability that is certain, death, is also neglected from a risk management and planning perspective, primarily due to most people not wanting to acknowledge their own mortality. To put a fine point on this, even the most wealthy, notable families are at risk of Financial Gravity due to negligence of Family Human Capital as it relates to death. J.D. Rockefeller was at one point said to be the world's first billionaire, and most likely the wealthiest man on the planet, who, in today's money, would make him the first trillionaire.

It is said that at the time of his death, 85% of his wealth was paid in taxes to the federal government. Even with that loss, it is estimated that he passed on over $15 billion in today's money to his descendants. The folklore is that no one asked him the question 'What planning have you done?' under the assumption that someone of his immense wealth had a plan across all Asset Silos.

Our folklore reality is that he hadn't done nearly enough to mitigate the liability of Federal Estate Taxes. That said, perhaps he knew exactly what he was doing, as the United States was on the verge of collapse during the

Great Depression when he died, and his taxes may have helped provide the means to maintain the American dream. Or perhaps he simply wanted to ensure that his descendants would have a reason to be productive members of society and find the same reward in building success that he did, trusting that he had adequately established the Family Emotional Governance to propagate his vision for generations to come.

The Total Family Balance Sheet Framework uniquely considers family human capital as a valuable asset. By assessing the family's skills, knowledge, and relationships, and by implementing proactive strategies to develop and nurture these assets, families can enhance their overall well-being and ensure their long-term financial success. This holistic approach recognizes that true wealth encompasses not only financial assets but also the intangible value of human capital, building a resilient and prosperous legacy for generations to come. Failing to value this asset is akin to ignoring a significant part of your family's overall net worth.

Checklist & Key Questions

- Have we clearly identified the core skills, strengths/weaknesses, and knowledge that each family member contributes or detracts from the family's long-term success?
- Are we intentionally developing future generations through education, mentorship, and exposure to meaningful personal and professional opportunities?
- Do we actively cultivate and protect the family's most valuable relationships, networks, and reputational assets?
- Have we established a clear structure for family governance that supports healthy communication, conflict resolution, and collective decision-making?
- Are we documenting and transferring institutional family knowledge, stories, values, processes, and lessons that future generations will need?

- Have we assessed the risks associated with gaps in family leadership, succession, or skill development, and created plans to address them?
- Do we have a strategy to ensure the family name, brand, and reputation are preserved and strengthened across generations?

Conclusion

The story of J.D. Rockefeller and his letters to his son is a powerful reminder that the most enduring legacy a family leaves is not its balance sheet, but its beliefs, behaviors, and culture. In those letters, Rockefeller stresses self-reliance, character, and personal responsibility, making it clear that while a family may provide a starting point, each individual's decisions ultimately shape their destiny. That same principle sits at the center of the Total Family Balance Sheet Framework: financial capital may open doors, but it is Family Human Capital, skills, judgment, values, governance, and culture, that determines whether those doors stay open for future generations.

By viewing family human capital as a deliberate asset class rather than an accidental byproduct of success, families can begin to invest and manage its inherent risks with the same rigor they apply to portfolios, operating companies, and their other Asset Silos. Thoughtful governance structures, intentional education and mentorship, clear expectations, and a shared sense of purpose all work together to resist Financial Gravity and keep the family moving forward rather than drifting apart. In the end, great multigenerational families look a lot like great multigenerational companies: they adapt, they learn, they honor their founding principles, and above all, they protect and perpetuate a strong culture. When Family Financial Governance and Family Emotional Governance are aligned, family human capital becomes the engine that sustains both wealth and meaning long after any single generation is gone.

PART III
IMPLEMENTING THE TOTAL FAMILY BALANCE SHEET

Now that we've explored the risks within each silo of the Total Family Balance Sheet, this final section turns toward implementation and integration. Here, we bring the entire framework to life, showing how to apply the four tools of risk management (Avoidance, Mitigation, Transference, or Assumption) across the family's entire financial ecosystem.

The six core silos are the Investment Portfolio, Real Estate, Family Operating Business, Private Equity, Personal Assets and Family Human Capital. Each presents unique risks and challenges. However, true resilience stems from understanding how these silos interact with one another.

The purpose of the Total Family Balance Sheet framework is to help you understand how factors such as risk frequency and severity shape your strategy, evaluate your family's true exposures, and make informed decisions based on your Emotional and Physical Risk Tolerance, that support long-term wealth preservation. With this approach, thoughtful planning becomes practical protection that can help strengthen your family for generations.

As a successful family, it is entirely understandable that you may never have encountered, let alone implemented, a comprehensive risk management strategy of this depth. Families who have created significant success often focus on opportunity, growth, and stewardship, not on the hidden structural vulnerabilities that accumulate over time. This type of integrated framework remains unfamiliar because it involves a level of complexity rarely addressed in traditional planning, demands advisors who are both exceptionally knowledgeable and selfless in their commitment, and requires those advisors to operate collaboratively and fully aligned with your family's values. It also calls for a degree of discipline, candor, and vulnerability within the family and advisory team that is uncommon in most planning environments, along with a multi-generational commitment to a process that continues to evolve as your family evolves. For all these reasons, encountering such a holistic approach for the first time is not a reflection of anything overlooked but rather a natural outcome of how rare and demanding this level of risk management truly is. This kind of comprehensive risk management approach is not about accumulating more; it is squarely focused on protecting what you have.

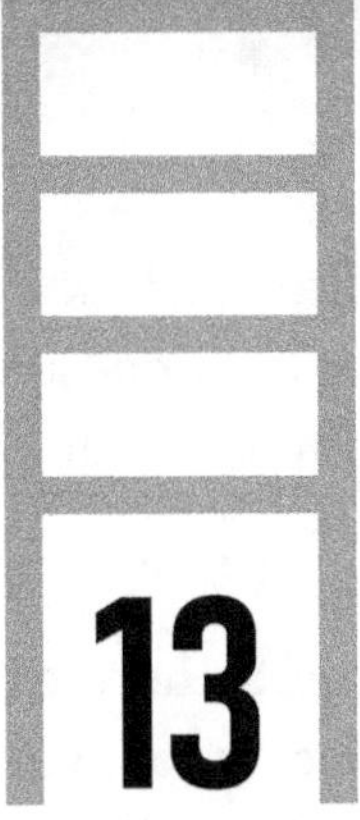

13

BUILDING A SUSTAINABLE LEGACY

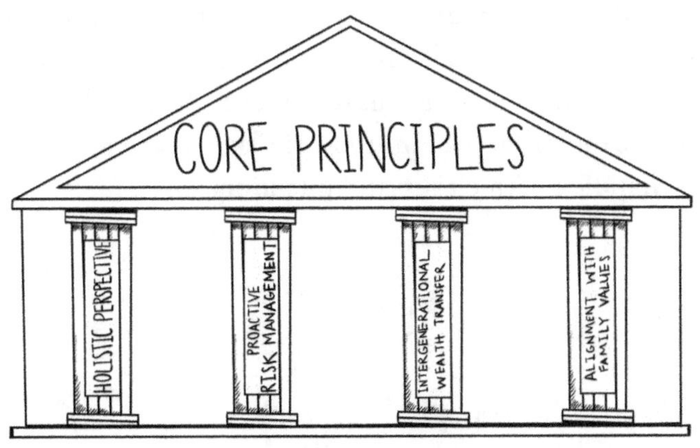

Figure 13.1 Core Principles of The Total Family Balance Sheet by Higginbotham™: A summary of the four core principles, holistic view, Informed risk evaluation, intergenerational wealth transfer, and values alignment, that underpin sustainable wealth across generations using the four tools of risk management (Avoidance, Mitigation, Transfer, or Assumption).

As we conclude this exploration of *The Total Family Balance Sheet by Higginbotham™*, it is essential to emphasize the core principles that underpin this revolutionary framework. *The Total Family Balance Sheet by Higginbotham™* represents a holistic approach to wealth preservation and risk management, recognizing that proper financial security lies not solely in asset accumulation but also in the strategic management of risks across all facets of a family's life. Throughout the chapters, we have emphasized the importance of addressing both on- and off-balance-sheet assets and liabilities, ensuring that families are equipped to handle the challenges they may face.

Holistic wealth and risk management recognize that every family's financial life is shaped by the interaction of many moving parts, diverse assets, evolving exposures, and both the visible and hidden liabilities that exist on and off the balance sheet. By adopting a comprehensive framework like the Total Family Balance Sheet, family's better position themselves to achieve long-term stability that extends far beyond simple financial growth. Proactively addressing risk, from frequent, low-severity disruptions to rare, high-severity events capable of altering a family's trajectory, is essential to resisting the persistent pull of Financial Gravity. This work begins with the family's intention and purpose to propagate wealth across generations by identifying all of a family's assets, understanding which risks are known and which remain unnoticed, then deliberately applying the appropriate tool from the four tools of risk management to ensure each exposure is handled with clarity and intention.

Figure 13.2 Prosperity & Purpose: The money tree representing the integrated growth of wealth and purpose, rooted in shared values. It symbolizes the strength of holistic wealth and risk management across generations.

Preparing the Family for the Work Ahead

A family begins the implementation phase by embracing the truth presented throughout the book that wealth preservation is not a passive outcome but the result of intentional and coordinated work. The six Asset Silos examined in earlier chapters represent the full landscape of a family's world. These include their Investment Portfolio, Real Estate, Family Operating Business, Private Equity holdings, Personal Assets and the vital category of Family Human Capital which shapes the judgment, readiness, governance structure, and culture that determine whether all other assets can endure.

The work of implementing the Total Family Balance Sheet begins by establishing the understanding that each family must adopt a comprehensive view of its exposures, drawing from the **Reframing Lens** introduced earlier in the book. This lens brings clarity to the interconnected nature of visible assets and hidden liabilities that exist both inside and outside the traditional balance sheet. Through this reframing process, the family begins to see not only what they own but also what they are exposed to.

The first actionable step is to gather the individuals who hold a meaningful role in the family's financial and emotional governance. The book emphasizes the importance of integrating all advisors and relevant voices into a shared understanding, rather than allowing fragmented decision-making to undermine long-term outcomes. These early meetings are designed to establish unity, clarity, and alignment.

The second step is to formally designate one person, or a small team, to be responsible for overall enterprise risk management. This role is not simply administrative. It requires clear authority and accountability to coordinate across asset silos, monitor exposures, validate that mandates are being followed, and ensure risk decisions remain aligned with the family's objectives and tolerance over time. Without an assigned risk leader, even well-intentioned plans can become inconsistent, reactive, or diluted across competing priorities.

This work establishes a foundation where the family can openly examine the gravitational forces that threaten long term wealth. The persistent pull of spending, taxes, litigation risk, misaligned incentives, market volatility, governance gaps, and unexamined exposures must all be brought into view so that the family can begin building protections strong enough to resist that force. The family must recognize that Financial Gravity is universal and does not discriminate based on net worth or intention. Only coordinated discipline can counter it.

While managing all these variables may feel exhausting, failing to do so can carry consequences of extraordinary magnitude. History makes this unmistakably clear. When we look at the Forbes 400 from 1982 and realize that only a small fraction of those families remains on the list today, it becomes evident how easily wealth can erode without deliberate, coordinated, and perpetual planning. The reality is that the less wealth a family has, the harder it is to hold on to, and even families with extraordinary means are not immune to Financial Gravity. Without a comprehensive framework like *The Total Family Balance Sheet by Higginbotham*™, the risk of losing what has been built, sometimes over decades or generations, grows exponentially. Although the work may seem difficult at times, standing strong and committing to the process is one of the most meaningful choices you can make. Your future self and your family will look back with gratitude for the discipline and intention you put in today.

A Closing Message for Families Beginning This Journey

As the book explains, the Total Family Balance Sheet Framework is a holistic approach to preserving wealth and managing risk with intention and clarity. It is not a tool to be picked up once and forgotten. It is a long term companion that grows stronger as the family becomes more informed, better coordinated, and more aligned in purpose.

You may feel a sense of disappointment that this book does not offer a simple directive or a neatly packaged set of instructions that says, in effect, now go do this. The irony, of course, is that no such book could ever exist. Every family's circumstances, values, dynamics, ambitions, and vulnerabilities are too distinct for any one-size-fits-all prescription. What can exist, and what this book aims to provide, is a framework: a way of thinking that enables your family to create its own evolving story as life changes. The work is not about following a script, but about engaging in a process that adapts as your family grows, encounters challenges, and discovers new opportunities.

This chapter concludes by affirming that the journey ahead is one of discipline, cooperation, curiosity, and shared stewardship. When the family honors the work by implementing the tools, understanding the silos, applying the Reframing Lens, and resisting Financial Gravity with coordinated action, they build a legacy more capable of standing for generations.

Now is the time to act. Don't wait for a crisis to reveal your blind spots. Your family is now prepared to begin.

GLOSSARY OF KEY TERMS

Total Family Balance Sheet Framework

- **Total Family Balance Sheet**
A holistic framework for evaluating and managing all assets, liabilities, and risks, both on- and off-balance-sheet, across a family's entire financial landscape.

- **Financial Gravity**
The natural pull that causes families to drift toward reactive, short-term decisions unless disciplined systems and governance are in place to counteract that pull.

- **Asset Silos**
Distinct asset categories within the family's holdings (e.g., investments, businesses, real estate, personal assets, human capital).

- **Off-balance-sheet-liabilities**
Risk exposures that are not traditionally tracked in financial statements but can significantly impact family wealth (e.g., litigation, reputation, cyber).

- **Holistic Risk Management**
An approach that integrates all sources of risk across silos to provide a comprehensive understanding of the family's vulnerability and resilience.

- **Integrated Risk Management**
Coordinating risk oversight across advisors and domains to eliminate blind spots and redundancy.

- **Reframing Lens**
  A structured way of looking at a situation from multiple angles to uncover blind spots, clarify assumptions, and strengthen decision-making across the Total Family Balance Sheet.

Risk Awareness and Tolerance

- **Informed / Ill-Informed / Uninformed Risk Awareness**
  - *Informed*: Know the risk and have a strategy.
  - *Ill-Informed*: Assume protection or understanding where none exists.
  - *Uninformed*: Completely unaware of potential exposure.
- **Risk Tolerance**
  A family's capacity and willingness to absorb loss.
  - *Physical Risk Tolerance*: The objective financial ability to withstand loss.
  - *Emotional Risk Tolerance*: The psychological comfort with loss and uncertainty.
- **Risk Appetite Profiles**
  - *Risk-Averse*: Prioritizes safety and preservation.
  - *Risk-Neutral*: Balances risk and reward objectively.
  - *Risk-Seeking*: Accepts high risk in pursuit of high returns.

Risk Strategy Tools

- **Four Risk Management Strategies**
  - *Avoid:* Avoidance eliminates the exposure altogether.
  - *Mitigate:* Mitigation reduces likelihood or severity.
  - *Transfer:* Transference shifts risk to others (e.g., insurance, legal structures).
  - *Assume*: Assumption accepts the risk knowingly and plans accordingly.
- **Foundational Risk Approach**
  Prioritizing risk planning based on actual probability and potential consequences, not assumptions or habits.

- **Inverted Risk Focus**
  The common, flawed tendency to overprotect against unlikely risks while neglecting highly probable ones.

Risk Categories

- **Financial Risk**
  Market loss, liquidity crises, or underinsurance.
- **Legal Risk**
  Litigation, regulatory exposure, fiduciary breaches.
- **Operational Risk**
  Failures in systems, infrastructure, or day-to-day operations.
- **Strategic Risk**
  Poor decisions around growth, innovation, or competitive positioning.
- **Reputational Risk**
  Damage to brand, credibility, or trust, often with lasting impact.

Severity and Frequency

- **Frequency and Severity of Loss**
  A critical classification of risk of loss based on a personalized profile in risk management.
  - *High Frequency / Low Severity:* Minor, recurring losses (e.g., maintenance, small claims).
  - *High Frequency / High Severity:* Frequent, catastrophic losses (e.g., trucking company fleet exposure).
  - *Low Frequency / High Severity:* Rare, catastrophic losses (e.g., natural disasters, major lawsuits).
  - *Low Frequency / Low Severity:* Minor, uncommon losses (e.g., overflowing toilet*).*
- **Actuarial Anomaly**
  The concept that repeated low-severity events can mask or even increase vulnerability to high-severity events due to desensitization or complacency.

Other Key Terms

- **Interest Rate Shock**
  Sudden changes in interest rates that adversely affect borrowing or investment performance.
- **Illiquidity Crisis**
  Inability to access cash or sell assets without significant loss.
- **Social Inflation**
  The rising cost of claims due to changing societal attitudes, litigation trends, and jury behavior.
- **Nuclear Verdicts**
  Substantial court awards that exceed traditional thresholds, often due to emotional jury responses.
- **Litigation Finance**
  Third-party funding of lawsuits in exchange for a portion of any potential settlement.
- **Insurance Guaranty Fund Limits**
  State-level backstops for failed insurers, often with limits that may fall short of claims.
- **Named-Peril vs. All-Risk Insurance Coverage**
  - *Named-Peril:* Covers only specifically listed risks.
  - *All-Risk:* Covers all risks unless explicitly excluded.
- **Risk Manager**
  An individual or advisor charged with identifying, evaluating, and coordinating risk management strategies across all asset classes and silos.

www.ingramcontent.com/pod-product-compliance
Lightning Source LLC
LaVergne TN
LVHW052148060426
835668LV00019B/2276